Ever So Slightly

Ever So Slightly

MARIAN
FLANDRICK
BRAY

Augsburg ▪ Minneapolis

EVER SO SLIGHTLY
Marian Flandrick Bray

Lyrics from "The Question," words and music by Justin Hayward,
copyright © 1970 Tyler Music Ltd., London, are reprinted on pages
55 and 91 by permission of TRO–Essex Music International, Inc., New
York.

Cover design and illustration: Catherine McLaughlin

Library of Congress Cataloging-in-Publication Data

Bray, Marian Flandrick, 1957–
  Ever so slightly / Marian Flandrick Bray.
     p. cm.
  Summary: Chronicles the growing friendship between two
runners on the school track team, Malena, a Christian severing
her ties with her former gang, and Bruce, a sixteen-year-old father
raising his baby by himself.
  ISBN 0-8066-2536-8 (alk. paper)
  [1. Unmarried fathers—Fiction.   2. Teenage parents—Fiction.
3. Track and field—Fiction.   4. Friendship—Fiction.   5.
Christian
life—Fiction.]   I. Title.
PZ7.B7388Ev   1990
[Fic]—dc20   91-12469
                                                       CIP
                                                        AC

The paper used in this publication meets the minimum requirements
of American National Standard for Information Sciences—Permanence
of Paper for Printed Library Materials, ANSI Z329.48-1984. ∞™

Manufactured in the U.S.A.   AF 9-2536

95   94   93   92   91   1   2   3   4   5   6   7   8   9   10

*To Greg Rathbun
who is changing ever so slightly
and to Chris von der Lieth
who is my Yolanda*

Thanks to Dave Lambert

CHAPTER 1

Malena

THE STARTING GUN exploded at the beginning of the practice race and Malena shifted into stride, smooth and fast. She was always amazed at how quickly her mind transformed from a good, logical high school sophomore who excelled in mathematics—her teachers' words, not just her own conceit, though there was that, too—to a wild, unfettered creature, running for the sheer joy of it.

One of the junior guys, Matt, accelerated past her. He'd die out before the end of this race. He always did. Malena relaxed her stride until she settled into the middle of the pack of runners. Five guys and her. Let Matt hold the lead. She didn't like running in front for the whole two miles. The stress of it was great, yes, but she didn't like not being able to see what the others were up to. In other words, she knew better than to trust a pack of guys, especially guys who didn't like being beaten by a girl.

She knew the guys thought of her as a freak. That saved their pride. They probably thought of her as someone devoid of gender, neither female nor male. She laughed to herself and wished it were so, if only to simplify her life.

Coach Wu hollered their times at the mile as they flashed by. His voice—loud, shrill, nasal—was like a Chinese torture.

She floated by him, not paying attention to the minutes and seconds but only using the numbers as sharp little spurs to urge her on.

As she rounded the far turn on the fifth lap, she sensed someone moving up beside her. Before she knew who it was, she guessed it was Bruce. But then usually Bruce Evans made his bid about now, at the mile and a quarter.

His pale blond hair flattened back, he looked like one of those slim Russian wolfhounds on vodka billboards. If it weren't for Malena, Bruce would be the fastest long distance runner at Southside High. She didn't know how he felt about that. If she were him, she'd be kind of jealous about it, but he never joined in on the crass remarks about her.

In fact, he seemed almost transparent at times, like he wasn't there, like a pale ice cube dropped into the boiling water of this miserable high school. She only saw him at track workouts, never during school, never in the halls. Of course, he was a grade ahead of her, and it was a huge high school, but still. . . .

Earlier that morning, before school, when Malena had been explaining math homework to her younger sister, Lucia, she thought of Bruce. She had tried explaining integer numbers—whole numbers. Lucia had still looked blank. "You know," Malena had told her, "not fractions, a complete thing."

Bruce had flickered to mind because she sensed he was a whole number, not fragmented like some people, like her ex-friends, Nadine and Annie. But once even they had been whole numbers, hadn't they?

Get a grip, she told herself, mentally shaking off the distraction. *You do come up with the strangest things.*

She ran on, emptying her mind of whole numbers, fractions, everyone, everything, all to be dealt with later. She just ran with Bruce Evans dogging her heels and the junior guy still in front. She drew breath after breath of the burning, smoggy air.

On the homestretch of the seventh lap, she smoothly pulled into the lead, Bruce still pounding behind her. Coach Wu shrieked their times and waved both arms, his version of "all's well."

One lap to go. Malena gathered herself for the final kick. From the finish line, Coach Wu shrieked in Chinese, holding his stop watch over his balding head like a knife. Maybe he hoped to slice time.

Something brushed her arm. Startled, she looked back. Bruce was leaning too far forward. His dark blue eyes widened, surprised. He stumbled—no, he was falling. Instinctively, Malena put out her hand to catch him. He shied out of her way. She could read in his face, No, you don't have to fall, too.

Bruce went down, his hands breaking his fall. Surprised shouts rose up from the pack behind them.

Malena slowed and jumped over the curb onto the grassy infield. Coach Wu's voice stung her like a whip, still in Chinese, but some things didn't need translating. She very nearly obeyed and straightened up, but something held her back.

A whole number had fallen.

She stopped dead. Then she turned and stepped out onto the track again. Bruce was on his knees, wiping his nose with his wrist, then, wiping his gritty hands on his shorts. Little flecks of blood clung to his thin white tee shirt. His blond hair was so fair that he looked almost bald until the light caught the gleam of pale gold.

"Are you okay?" Her breath was short and her heart was hammering, her body confused, wondering why she wasn't still running. The body knew the distances and knew it wasn't time to stop.

Bruce swore loudly and elegantly. Malena knelt down on the sandy track. If she'd sworn those words, her friend Rudy would have fined her $3.50. Bruce sat back on his heels. "I never fall," he said finally. "What happened?"

Malena couldn't tell him.

Coach Wu crossed the grass, his face red.

She stepped closer. "Can you get up?" she asked. Bruce smelled of salt and blood and dirt.

He sat back on his haunches like a puppy, then stood, swayed a moment, then stiffened and stayed upright. "I'm fine," he said to Malena. "Really. I guess I tripped." His voice switched from hesitating to confident. But she didn't believe his voice. She believed his eyes, which still registered shock.

Coach Wu strode over to them. "What happened?" He wore nylon sweatsuits, and all his moves swished with the smooth material. He stood, legs spread, one fist balled up, the other clenching the stopwatch.

Bruce shrugged and studied his palms. Blood welled up in beads along the scrapes.

"You, young woman," said Coach Wu, pointing at Malena with a thick forefinger. "You do not stop during a race."

Malena flinched. She knew.

Bruce's gaze touched her, and she met his eyes for a moment. He opened his mouth—to say thanks? leave me alone? what?

Then Coach Wu whirled on Bruce, firing questions. "Did you eat breakfast? Eat Lunch? You sick? Getting enough sleep?" On and on he ranted until Malena had to turn from the bullet questions and walk across the infield, past the pack, who teased her. "We beat you, little chili pepper." She suddenly hated them for missing the point entirely.

But she hated herself, too, because her feelings snarled and scattered into little points, and she wasn't sure which *was* the real point.

CHAPTER 2

Bruce

BRUCE WATCHED Malena walk back across the field, her head up, ignoring the usual barrage of insults from other team members. Coach Wu's questions passed over his head like the wind. He couldn't think of any suitable answers.

Finally, the coach was quiet, studying him thoughtfully, as if Bruce had suddenly transformed into something odd. "Go clean up, Evans," the coach finally said. "You look like Tiananmen Square survivor."

At least he looked like a survivor.

Bruce took off, hoping to avoid the other guys. He didn't want to answer their questions, either. He grabbed his backpack, crossed the football field and track, and shot out through the chain-link fence onto the street to head for the sitter's to pick up the baby. A shadow moved. He jumped as Malena stepped out of the long shadows cast by the evergreen hedge behind the chain-link fence.

Her feet were bare; she held her running shoes in her hand. The rest of her stuff bulged in a backpack slung over one shoulder.

"Hi," she said. Then, stating the obvious, she added, "I waited for you."

Bruce was puzzled. Basically, he'd sworn off girls after Juliana. Not that he was going to be a monk or anything, but he had to have some distance. His uncle had told him that was a good idea. When Zachary was born, Bruce was afraid the baby would always remind him that he shouldn't have messed around with girls, specifically Juliana. But somehow Zachary never did remind him of that. Maybe because the baby was someone who existed on his own and that was all.

"Walking home?" Malena asked. "I'll walk part way with you."

He nodded, not wanting to be rude. He was curious, after all. He walked, teetering on the edge of the curb, not wanting to walk too close to Malena.

She lightly swung her racing shoes and crunched through curved leaves from the eucalyptus trees, moving like a little brown creature. Her eyes were large and dark. Even the side part in her hair showed brown scalp.

Malena stepped along, not saying anything more, seemingly at peace while he grew more tense. He couldn't imagine what she'd want. More about him falling? Nice she was concerned, but hey, falls happen, right? They crossed Mission Avenue on the yellow light, running.

When they slowed on the sidewalk, Bruce asked, "So why did you wait for me?" The wind came up under his chin, cool and fresh, smelling of the Rio Hondo flood control, sage, and wet dirt.

"Because I wanted to know if you were really all right," she answered.

"Why?" he asked, but he meant, Why now? You've never cared before. He could tell by the way she jerked slightly that she had caught his meaning.

"You're my best competition, you know. You can't be failing on me now," she said, smiling a little. "You know what they say about your enemy spurring you on to greater heights."

Bruce laughed. He couldn't help it. Fiery little Malena thinking he was an enemy!

"So tell me what's happening." Her voice was quiet.

Suddenly, he did want to tell her, not just anyone, but her, Malena. "I guess it's mostly because I'm tired. I have a six-month-old baby, and he takes up a lot of time. Like he wakes up at night." Just thinking about it, Bruce stifled a yawn, his hand to his mouth. His palm stung from the fall.

"Oh, that's right," she said carefully. "I'd heard."

He guessed she'd heard. Juliana probably told all five thousand kids at Southside what a jerk he was. But he wondered what Malena thought about him keeping Zachary. Most kids thought he was nuts.

"I remember when you dropped out of cross country," she said, shaking her hair back out of her eyes. "I figured it was because of the kid."

"Yeah," he said, not sure how much to tell her or how much she wanted to know. Cars roared by, headed deeper into Los Angeles.

"I'm glad you could come back to track." She paused.

He knew his cue. "My uncle is helping me out. The baby is at a babysitter's. We thought that it would be best if I could keep up with all the stuff I had been doing before Zachary." That was kind of how he thought of his life: before Zachary, after Zachary. The transformation had been sudden and complete.

Malena's gaze was on his face. "I thought about you this morning," she said. "Maybe I knew something was happening to you."

"Like ESP?" He tried to remember exactly what he did this morning.

"More like God nudged me and said, 'Hey, pay attention to Bruce today.' "

Bruce chuckled. "I don't mind God talking as long he doesn't start hurtling lightning bolts."

Malena smiled. "I don't think God's quite like that."

"Are you sure?"

She nodded. "Yeah. Well, most of the time."

They walked to the corner of Jackson and Fifth, where the streets began to change, turn feral, moving into the barrios.

"I go this way," Malena said, pointing across the busy intersection. She waved and crossed at the light, heading toward the Jardín, the Garden. Practically every Hispanic kid lived in the Garden, but the Jardín wasn't a flower garden. In fact, a kid once told him that Jardín was a play on words, that on a boat the Spanish word meant a privy, a toilet.

Bruce jogged to Nina's house—the babysitter's—at the foot of the swell of hills that led up to where the richer people—mostly white—lived. He lived up there, too, with Uncle Justin—ever since his parents had kicked him out.

CHAPTER 3

Malena

"TAKE A SHOWER!" Malena's brother hollered from the couch. Eleven-year-old Ramon was the next oldest to her and resented it deeply. She knew he thought he ought to have been the firstborn since he was a boy and supposedly more highly regarded for that fact. She suspected, however, that she was Papa's favorite, even though Papa would never admit it.

"Oh, shut up," she said, shaking her running shoes in his face. Track dirt flecked off and fell onto his light blue shirt.

Ramon yelped and took a swing at her.

But she was too quick. She backed out of his way. *"Toro, toro,"* she chanted, holding the shoes before him like a cape.

He yelled and swatted at her shoes. He missed and leaped off the couch after her. Malena, laughing, ran to her bedroom and slammed the door behind her. Ramon crashed against it, like the maddened, black fighting bulls of Spain.

Inside the room she shared with her sister, Malena held the door shut with her shoulder until Ramon roared off. Lucia, her nine-year-old sister, sat at a card table in the corner of the room. The flat table was decorated with colored bits of clay houses and animals—a whole world in modeling clay.

"You scared me," said Lucia, a limp roll of green clay like a string bean in her hand. "I thought it was another earthquake."

The bedsprings groaned as Malena sat down and un-loaded her backpack. An earthquake had rumbled through Southside two nights before—4.9 on the Richter scale, the epicenter in Pico Rivera, less than three miles away.

The jolter had knocked all her math and astronomy books off her shelf and broke the net holding Lucia's stuffed animals, tumbling them all over the floor.

In the dark crashing, Lucia had whimpered. Malena dragged her sister out from under the covers and under the door frame, supposedly the safest place to be, ac-cording to all the earthquake preparedness pamplets the school was forever passing out. But Malena doubted the wisdom of it. In their house anyway.

"No earthquake," Malena said. "Just Ramon, the little pest."

"Did you know my friends at school think Ramon's cute?" asked Lucia.

"Cute?" Malena stared at her sister. "Are your friends blind?"

Lucia threw the piece of green clay. It missed Malena and smacked against the wall. Malena picked it up and rolled it between her palms.

"Don't insult my friends," said Lucia.

Malena fell back on her bed. As she thought about her brother, she couldn't think of anything cute about him. Sometimes he showed a flash of his good side. But that was as rare as a Metal Jungle gang member going to church. "God help us," she said to the ceiling.

"You shouldn't use God's name in vain," said Lucia. She bobbed her head like old Father Gomez did when he was reading from the Old Testament about some punishment that God had zapped to the Israelites.

But Malena had told Bruce that God didn't unleash lightning bolts on people. He used to, though, didn't he? She'd have to think about that one.

"I'm sorry," said Malena automatically, even though she meant what she had said. God forbid that girls should think her brother was cute. Malena wondered if God minded because she really did mean it and wasn't swearing.

"You *should* be sorry," said Lucia.

She wasn't, but she restrained her words. Her little sister was in her legalistic mode. Mama said that it was a phase that kids went through.

Ignoring her sister, she flipped open her notebook and began a letter to *Tia* Kate. Well, Kate wasn't really her aunt, but a cousin. But because Kate was seven years older, Malena called her aunt.

She wrote:

Dear Tia Kate,

A weird thing happened today. No, two weird things. This guy I run track with fell down during a race. He was okay, but we talked. He has a baby. Can you imagine? He's only a junior.

She chewed on her pen cap. *What would make a guy keep his baby?* Rumor had it that his ex-girlfriend had wanted an abortion, but he talked her out of it so he could have the baby. Why? Why would a guy want a baby?

She chewed on the pen a minute, then wrote some more.

Another weird thing happened today. Well, not so weird because it's more common these days. Nadine and Annie are being horrible. They act like they don't like Yolanda and me. Like today—

Malena stopped writing. Today the four of them had been sitting and eating lunch outside in the junior-senior park under an ancient oak tree. Oak trees were supposed to hold magical qualities, but maybe the magic didn't work in the city because what happened was not magical.

Get real, Malena, she told herself. *Magic? You're a scientist and a Christian.* But she did believe in magic. Desperately. She believed in God's magic.

At lunch she'd mostly been talking to Yolanda, who was her very best friend, when Nadine had said, "Here comes Jordan. What a babe."

Nadine opened her flat, black purse, fished for a tube of brick red lipstick and began applying it.

Jordan walked along the cracked sidewalk with two other guys from varsity football. Even though football season was long over, the players were still worshiped wherever they went. Malena hated that. What was football? A bunch of dumb guys running over each other. She sighed and bit into her apple.

Nadine shoved her lipstick back in her purse and stood, her black skirt short. Her legs were great looking. Nadine knew it and made sure everyone else noticed, too. Malena crunched her apple unhappily.

"Where are you going, Nadine?" Annie asked. She fluttered to her feet.

"I don't want Jordan to think I hang around with you guys," Nadine said.

Yolanda merely pushed her glasses up higher on her nose.

Malena bristled. "What the hell does that mean, Nadine?" *Ching!* Fifty cents to her friend Rudy for swearing.

"Well, I don't mean it personally," said Nadine. She flicked her hair back, waiting to pounce on Jordan. Malena knew how she worked. She'd seen Nadine pounce a hundred times.

"Just how do you mean it if it isn't personal?" asked Yolanda.

"I want Jordan to think I'm more, you know. . . ." Nadine's voice trailed off as Jordan approached. He grinned and winked at Nadine, who smiled back. "Hi, Jordan," she said.

Annie moved in beside Nadine, still fluttering like a baby crow.

Malena wanted to throw her apple core at Jordan's head. No, not him, at Nadine. "You want Jordan to think you're more what?" Malena demanded. She sat rigid, her backbone like ice. "You want him to think you're more stupid? More asinine? More idiotic? More what, Nadine?"

At his name Jordan glanced over at Malena and winked at her.

Nadine scowled, the bright lipstick a slash. "Try more mature," Nadine hissed.

"That must be a new experience." Malena lifted her chin, scowling back.

Nadine simply turned and walked up to Jordan, her heels clicking on the uneven sidewalk. Annie gave Malena a funny, oblique look, then hurried after Nadine and Jordan. The two varsity players and Annie trailed behind like lost children.

Malena threw her apple core to the waiting gulls who screamed and swooped, fighting for the fruit. Their white and gray wings beat the air. She and Yolanda silently picked up their trash from lunch, as well as Nadine and Annie's, dropped them in the trash can, and walked silently to their lockers. Anger burned through Malena until she knew how stars must feel, their bellies burning with the hot fury of fusion.

Malena sighed and finished her letter to Tia Kate. Then she left her room to get an envelope. Ramon was watching television—some dumb cartoon—and hardly stirred.

Mama was in the kitchen with Carlos, the baby of the family at seven years old. Mama stirred a pot of pinto beans over the stove. For a moment Malena thought about telling Mama about Nadine and Annie, but Carlos began talking about school, and Malena didn't want to interrupt him.

Instead, she went out back to their tiny yard and stood in the soft, falling darkness and counted the stars. She counted just five and bright Saturn, burning through the smog. Some nights no stars showed.

Anger still burned in her stomach from lunch time— no, it had been there for a long time. Suddenly, she realized that her belly fire wasn't the heat of stars' fusion, because that was joyous. No, this feeling was cold. It burned like the frozen realms of space. Teeth-grinding cold, lump-of-frozen-ice cold, and worst of all, the cold of being alone. That was her anger.

CHAPTER 4

Bruce

BRUCE WARMED a bottle of formula for Zachary. Uncle Justin wasn't home yet because he usually saw his dental patients until six and sometimes did paperwork before he came home. Zachary lay on Bruce's lap, his nose running. The baby screwed up his face, crying in loud, no-nonsense tones.

"Okay, okay. I can only warm this up so fast, kid," said Bruce. He bounced Zachary until the baby stopped crying for a millisecond. Bruce tested the milk's temperature, then popped the bottle in the baby's mouth. At first Zachary was crying so hard he didn't even know the nipple was there.

Soon he would. Where did the kid get his temper? From Juliana. She had a temper like nobody else.

Bruce opened his world civ book, found the right page, and waited for Zachary to latch onto the nipple. Bruce tried to read among the screams. Not easy. Finally the baby quieted and with wet eyes stared up at Bruce and drank.

"Stubborn kid, aren't you?" Bruce asked. But he was glad because stubbornness was important. If Bruce hadn't been stubborn, the baby wouldn't be there.

Literally.

When Juliana realized she was pregnant, she was nearly three months along.

"How could you not know?" Bruce had asked.

"Because I've never been pregnant before! Because my periods have never been regular! And since you're such an expert, how did I even get pregnant?"

The irony was that she'd been on the pill.

"You probably skipped taking it," he'd said.

"No way! I never forgot."

The doctor had said it wasn't the first time someone got pregnant on the pill. Juliana wanted an abortion, but her mother had said that she'd kick Juliana out if she did.

At first Bruce had assumed an abortion would be the best thing. Her mom wouldn't really kick her out of the house. Her parents doted on her too much. Getting an abortion would solve everything. But then it preyed on him, especially at night, lying in bed. This wasn't just a bunch of tissue. He would be killing his own child. It terrified him. His parents and friends had thought he was completely bonkers.

They still did.

So he and Juliana's mother talked Juliana out of having an abortion. Juliana seethed and refused to see him anymore. Which was just as well. But still, it was difficult. Now the baby was his.

He looked down at Zachary, still feeding, the bubbles streaking up through the plastic bottle. Maybe he was crazy, but he was glad that he had gotten the baby.

The front door slammed. "Hey," called Uncle Justin as he walked in, carrying his worn briefcase. Zachary liked Uncle Justin's briefcase. He would often gum the handles and sometimes he would scream until one of them opened the briefcase and let him drool on the plaster casts of teeth Uncle Justin carried inside the case.

"How's it going?" asked Bruce.

"Oh, fairly well," said Uncle Justin. "We rescued a kid's front teeth." He set down his briefcase and patted Zachary's swelling belly. The baby ignored him and concentrated on drinking. Uncle Justin went on. "The kid was playing hardball and got hit in the face."

"Geez," said Bruce. He looked down at the baby. "Don't play hardball, Zachary." The baby ignored him, too, and kept drinking.

"But we saved them. Smart teacher packed the teeth on ice right away. But it was a wild afternoon for the kid and me."

Uncle Justin was a thin version of Bruce's father. Tall, with blond hair, though Dad's was gray now. They had the same almond-shaped, gray-blue eyes, and a thin-lipped mouth. On Uncle Justin it was a friendly smile, but on Dad it was aggressive. Uncle Justin and Dad were fifteen years apart, and the generation gap was wide and yawning.

"Have you eaten?" asked Uncle Justin.

Bruce shook his head.

Uncle Justin began making dinner, taking out frozen chicken and tossing it in the microwave, washing vegetables and chopping them on the drainboard. Bruce tried to finish reading his world civ while Zachary nuzzled his bottle.

A few pages into world civ, Uncle Justin interrupted him. "Your father called me this morning."

Bruce carefully kept his face still. "What did he want?"

"The same old stuff. Wondering if you've gotten tired of Zachary yet."

Yes. No. Of course he was tired of the baby. It was hard work. But he wasn't going to give up. Zachary was halfway through the bottle, so Bruce lifted the baby over his shoulder.

Zachary gave a protesting yelp.

"Tough, kiddo," said Bruce. The baby settled down as Bruce patted his back. "What did you tell him?" asked Bruce.

"What I always tell him. To call you and ask you."

Bruce smiled wryly. "He didn't take your advice."

"He rarely does. He's a stubborn man."

Interesting word choice. Like father, like son, like grandson. Dad wouldn't like to hear that, though.

Zachary gave a loud burp.

"My sentiments as well," said Uncle Justin.

Early that morning Mom had called, not Dad. She usually called a few times a week. For some reason he never mentioned it to Uncle Justin.

Mom always said basically the same stuff. "I wanted to catch you before school."

"Well, you did." He was such a brilliant conversationalist.

"How are you?" she asked.

He imagined his mother, tall, fashionably slim, with expensive frosted hair, long pink nails. People said he inherited her looks. The fine, thin-arched nose, large blue eyes, same body type. Mom could have been a runner.

"I'm okay," he said. Their last conversation hadn't gone well. She'd started crying, then Zachary had started screaming. Just to be sure that didn't happen again, Bruce cradled the phone between his neck and shoulder while he fixed a bottle and gave it to Zachary. He told Mom the brief details. Races won. Tests coming up. Grades, mostly B's. He didn't tell her he had a C– in chemistry.

"How's the baby?"

Always *the baby*. Never Zachary. Bruce had picked the name from Dad and Uncle Justin's father, the grandfather he never had known.

"Zachary is fine. I'm giving him his bottle right now. I hope he'll start sleeping through the night soon."

"I wish I could see him." Her voice sounded like a little girl's.

"Come over and visit." He said that every time. She was quiet a moment. Upstairs, Uncle Justin was walking around, the floorboards squeaking. Zachary sucked on the bottle and stared up at Bruce, like he was in love with him, which, according to the baby books, was just about true.

With his forefinger Bruce stroked Zachary's fine, soft hair.

"Oh, your father is out of the shower. I better get going."

"Okay, Mom." Geez, the Eastern bloc countries never had it so bad. For her the Berlin wall was still up.

"I miss you," she said. Then she hung up.

He always felt bad when she said that because he didn't miss them. At least not the situation—his father refusing to talk to him because of the baby. He missed having his parents back him up. That's what he missed.

Now Bruce shifted the baby to his other shoulder. "I fell down during practice today," he told Uncle Justin. He held up one skinned hand.

Uncle Justin stood over him, smelling of antiseptic. "What happened?"

"Tired, I think. Usually when I'm running, I don't think a lot. I just run." Bruce laid the baby back in the crook of his arm and let Zachary finish the last dregs of his bottle. "But Zachary woke up three times last night. I think I was sort of sleep running. I had this dream that I couldn't take care of Zachary, go to school, and do all the stuff I was supposed to. In my dream I collapsed. Then today I really did fall down."

Uncle Justin sat in a chair opposite him, stroking his pale mustache thoughtfully. "Well, I'm not a psychiatrist, but I think I get your meaning. Sometimes I feel like falling down, too. I'm afraid if I did, my patients would be even more nervous than they are."

Bruce smiled at that. Uncle Justin had a couple of people who needed sedatives before they could get their teeth worked on. They reminded him of his family's old Sheltie, Kiwi, who had to be tranquilized before they took her to the vet's.

"So what do you do so you don't fall down?" asked Bruce.

There was a long silence as Uncle Justin stroked his mustache again. Bruce imagined all kinds of philosophical answers like, You have to be strong because people are depending on you, or Don't even think about failing or it'll be a self-fulfilling prophesy.

Uncle Justin merely stood and walked over to the sink to finish making salads. "I'm still working on that answer, Bruce," he said. "I'm not sure except to keep trying. And when you fall down, you get back up."

Bruce looked down at Zachary. The baby dozed over the nearly empty bottle. "Oh no, you don't, kid," said Bruce. "You wake up now. I don't want to be up all night again with you." He jiggled the baby awake.

As he looked into Zachary's smoky blue eyes, he wondered, *But what if you fall down and you can't get back up anymore?*

CHAPTER 5

Malena

Malena

AFTER DINNER, as Malena worked on her trigonometry homework, the phone rang. She didn't bother pausing. It wasn't usually for her. So she kept swimming among numbers and equations.

Papa called to her, "For you, Malena."

The numbers slipped through her fingers like water. She shoved back her chair and got the phone in the kitchen. Sometimes Yolanda called her from a phone booth. Lucia was standing on a chair, leaning over the sink, finishing the dishes. Malena pressed against the humming refrigerator. "Hello?"

"This is Annie."

"Yeah?" Malena asked slowly.

"We're meeting tomorrow night at McDonald's to discuss some business," said Annie. "Be there."

Was that a threat or what? Malena nearly laughed, but instead she said, "Why?"

Annie just said, "Hey, we saw you with Pops."

"What?" Then she realized Annie was talking about Bruce. "So what's it to you?"

"It's just really disgusting." Annie's voice sounded funny, like she was either trying to keep from laughing or was disguising her voice. But then Annie was always trying on new selves.

Malena was never sure if Annie just didn't like herself or was just so superficial that she shifted personas like changes of clothes.

Annie said. "I mean, he knocks up a girl, then keeps her kid. Really low of you to hang out with him."

No, people like you are low, Malena thought. "Look, Annie, say what you gotta say, okay? I've got homework to do."

"You just show up at McDonald's. You've been warned." The phone slammed down, and the dial tone blared.

Malena stared at the receiver. "I'm scared," she said sarcastically. Then she hung up the phone in disgust.

"What's the matter?" asked Lucia, pausing from blowing soap bubbles through her fingers.

Malena didn't know how to say it simply. "Nadine makes Annie do stupid things." Annie was such a puppet.

Malena stomped back to her room. It was a long time before the cold anger burned down enough so that she could immerse herself in her numbers again.

CHAPTER 6

Bruce

AFTER TRACK WORKOUT the next dat, Bruce glanced around for Malena, but she was gone already, so he picked up his sweats and started home. He decided it would be easier to shower at home and drop off his stuff, then go pick up Zachary at Nina's.

Nina had been a dental hygienist with Uncle Justin's practice but stayed home after her baby was born. She said she could use the money so agreed to watch Zachary. She seemed nice, and he never heard her yell at the kids. He liked that.

Bruce walked down the street, the high school behind him. At track today Malena had only said hello to him and looked far away. He hardly knew her and yet he'd hoped—

Hoped what?

Remember, no girls, Bruce. Think. Remember what happened when you got involved with a girl? Not that he'd wish Zachary into nonexistence, though he wouldn't have minded putting Zachary off for a few years—like ten maybe.

He turned the corner. Behind him rumbled a familiar car's engine, moving slower than a car should be moving on this street. He looked over his shoulder. A white Camaro purred up behind him. Girl driving. Juliana.

She pulled next to him. "Want a ride?" she called through the open passenger's window. She was alone, which he found odd because she'd been flaunting her new boyfriend. What was his name? Derek something. A thin, tall guy with dark blond hair to his shoulders.

"No thanks," Bruce called back, trying to sound casual. Getting into her car one too many times had been exactly his problem.

"Come on, Bruce," she said. "I just want to talk with you. I'll take you home." She leaned across the seat to open the passenger door, her low-cut blouse revealing. She smiled.

Juliana was being too friendly. He hesitated. No, how could someone be too friendly? Shouldn't he get along with his child's mother? A sudden feeling like hitting a live wire surged into him.

Divorced parents must feel this way. It was like being shut in a dark room, not knowing where the door was, having to feel around, groping, alone, lost. . . .

Juliana pushed the passenger door open slightly. She was pretty, with long curly blond hair. And having the baby hadn't ruined her figure. She still looked good, very good. She sat back up, the car door still open.

"Come on. I'll give you a ride home, okay?" She tapped her long fingernails, red today, on the padded steering wheel.

He shook his head again. "I'll walk. I need the exercise. But thanks anyway." Something told him to walk on. His own guilty conscience? What had Malena said about God nudging her? Was that this feeling? But then why would God care if he talked with Juliana? Anyway, talking is not where they got into trouble.

Juliana frowned, wrinkling her forehead. "Bruce, come on." She always was demanding and pushy.

Still trying to be casual, he waved and moved on down the sidewalk. But he walked awkwardly, feeling caught, like a trapped insect.

The Camaro roared off.

Bruce pushed through late afternoon shadows tossed down by the oak trees. She didn't even wave good-bye. He blinked and could have sworn someone suddenly sat up in the back seat. The Camaro stopped at the end of the street, then swerved left onto Broadway, just avoiding a red Toyota pickup that honked.

A shadow must have slid into the car, looking like a person, he thought. He broke into a jog to leave behind his tangled emotions—for a few minutes anyway.

CHAPTER 7

Malena

OUTSIDE the large windows of McDonald's the night had laid down thick bands of gray over the city. Malena longed to be out in it. The night was infinitely more comforting than having to face Nadine and Annie. Next to her, Yolanda ordered fries and a chocolate shake.

"Diet Coke, large, please," said Malena.

The guy behind the counter gave her an eager smile. She knew him from last year's English class. He used to sit in her seat before class and tell her to sit in his lap. That got old. Fast.

"Hi, Malena. How's track?" he asked.

She couldn't even remember his name. "Just fine."

"Still beating the boys, huh?"

"Something like that." She held out two dollar bills.

He ran his fingers along her palm as he took the money. Her skin crawled.

Yolanda brushed her. "They're here," she said quietly. "Over in the back."

The guy handed Malena the change, his fingers touching her hand again, a second too long. Then he gave her the Diet Coke.

"Why is it," asked Malena as they walked into the dining room, "that the guys I could care less about won't leave me alone but the ones I like ignore me?"

"You're asking the wrong person, *muchacha*," said Yolanda. "I've never even been asked out."

"That's not true."

"Oh, please. My cousin does not count."

Malena laughed. "Don't feel bad. I've only gone out a few times."

"But you've been asked, at least."

Not by anyone she wanted. But the problem was, who did she want? There was one guy—Kyle Garrett. She'd met him at a camp the previous summer. Even though he lived in Orange County, not far from Southside, he was another world away.

Yolanda elbowed her. "We're young, no? We got lots of time, right?" she asked mockingly.

That's what people said, but Malena didn't feel so young.

They walked into the back of the restaurant where Nadine, Annie, and Jordan, the jock, filled a small booth. Malena was surprised to see Jordan. She had thought the meeting was girls only. She should have known better.

"How convenient," said Yolanda. "No room for us."

They shouldn't have come, Malena thought, but not going would have given Nadine more ammunition to get back at them. They couldn't win either way.

Some little kids twirled on tall, white stools at the counter along one wall, licking dripping ice cream cones and laughing and shouting together. Their mothers and fathers sat at the red round tables probably trying to forget they had kids.

Malena and Yolanda halted in front of the booth. Jordan had his arm around Nadine's shoulders. His cologne, a musky scent, reached out and netted Malena. She nearly sneezed.

Annie sat across from Nadine and Jordan. Annie, in a tight black sweater, swirled the straw in her Coke and said, "Hey."

Malena jerked her chin in greeting and let her gaze slide over to Nadine, who raised an eyebrow as if to say, So you're here. Big deal.

Malena and Yolanda sat across from their booth at a red round table, gritty with salt. Malena blew the salt onto the floor.

"Since when are the Little Ones taking on guys?" asked Yolanda, her voice loud enough for the others to hear.

Malena snapped, "The Little Ones are no more."

Nadine laughed, her voice like a plastic charm bracelet. "A good idea, no?"

Malena wasn't sure if Nadine meant a good idea to take on guys or that the Little Ones were no more.

"What's the Little Ones?" asked Jordan.

He could have been good looking except his blue eyes were empty. Malena could have pardoned it—too much head-banging in football, except he'd been vapid since she knew him in sixth-grade, pre-football days.

"The Little Ones is our gang," said Annie. She glanced over at Nadine, who frowned. Annie corrected herself. "I mean, it *was* our gang." She tossed back her burgundy-colored hair with long black roots showing.

Malena leaned back in her chair until it creaked.

"You used to be in a gang, huh?" said Jordan. "I like a woman who's feisty." He winked at Nadine.

What a donkey. If he knew the first thing about gangs, he wouldn't be so casual. He must not know Nadine's brother was the leader of the Metal Jungle gang. That was nothing to joke about. Malena wanted to throw her Coke at Jordan's stupid head.

"We were a nice gang," Yolanda was explaining. "We did good things."

Nadine sat forward. "But that was when we were kids. We're older now."

"Yeah," said Malena sarcastically. "I guess some of us outgrew doing good things and being Christians."

"You're such a fanatic," said Annie. "Get into the real world."

"What world do you belong to, jerk?" asked Malena.

Annie jumped up, bumping the table. The bag of fries jumped with her. "Outside, Malena."

It had been a long time since they'd had a good fist fight, but maybe it was time again. Malena threw down her straw. "It's not you I want. You're only a puppet. It's *her* I want." Malena pointed at Nadine, who stiffened and gave an embarrassed laugh.

"What's going on here?" asked Jordan through a mouthful of french fries.

Malena and Nadine didn't answer but stared at each other like snarling pitbulls. *Not like integer numbers,* thought Malena sadly. *Not whole numbers, but fractions.*

"Let's go, Malena," said Yolanda, pushing at her glasses. "Nothing here for us."

Malena shifted her feet over the gritty salt on the floor.

Nadine smiled her exotic cat smile and shook back her thick hair. "We didn't want you to come anyway," she said.

"We thought we were coming here to meet some *friends*," Malena said, her fingers turning cold.

Yolanda gathered up her food.

Annie sank back in her seat with a satisfied smile. "No one would be friends with you anyhow," she said.

Malena didn't answer but picked up her drink. They weren't worth fighting. She and Yolanda wove between tables halfway out of the restaurant when something hit her between the shoulder blades. An opened bag of catsup splatted on the floor. Malena whirled, furious. From the corner of the restaurant, Nadine and Annie whooped in laughter.

Yolanda wiped at Malena's back with a napkin. "It's not much, really," she said. "But you ought to wash it out so it doesn't stain."

Stain? Nadine was a stain. Malena wanted to wipe her out. She stalked back to the booth as Yolanda kept calling her name in little frightened bursts.

"I have a good aim, no?" called Nadine. Then she began laughing so hard that she buried her face in her arms on the table. Jordan still looked confused. He had his arm around Nadine, like an anchor.

Malena stopped at their table. "I have good aim, too," said Malena quietly. She dumped her entire Diet Coke on Nadine's head.

Coke and ice showered down. Nadine screamed. Jordan yelped and scooted sideways. The restaurant went silent, except a baby letting out a wail.

"My hair," cried Nadine, her voice shattering the stillness. She hopped up into the aisle and shook like a wet dog. Diet Coke and ice flew sideways. People began talking, shocked, calling out, wondering what happened, whether to be scared.

A man in a pin-striped suit and tie barrelled out of the kitchen and over to them. "What's going on here?" he demanded.

Malena ignored him and said to Nadine, "Don't mess with me again, *chica*." She stalked back down the aisle, stepping carefully over the broken catsup bag, Yolanda in her wake.

Customers murmured, like she'd stuck a knife in Nadine or something. She wanted to tell everyone how her friends were betraying her.

A couple of white guys laughed as she stomped by. "Hey, spicy salsa! I'll buy you another Coke!" one of them called.

She turned to blister him, but Yolanda pushed at her back. "Let's go."

"Don't you ever come back!" yelled the owner. He had a hand on Nadine's shoulder.

Disgusting.

Malena pushed on the glass front door and turned a moment to wait for Yolanda. Then she saw Bruce standing in line for food. He was holding a baby. Their eyes met. He was startled but seemed to catch himself and gave her a small smile.

Malena bolted.

CHAPTER 8

Bruce

AFTER SOMEONE SCREAMED, Malena had appeared at the front door, giving Bruce a shocked look. Then she fled. Zachary banged his hard head against Bruce's arm.

"I know that girl," said Bruce.

Uncle Justin looked up. "Creating a scene, isn't she?"

Malena and the other girl vanished outside, lost to the shadows and darkness.

"She's the one who beats me at track," he said. "She's usually quiet."

"I'll give her that. She's quietly causing trouble," said Uncle Justin. He took the tray with their food.

Malena wasn't a troublemaker, was she? Bruce had sensed a goodness, a center in her that not many others had. But maybe that was his wishful thinking. Why shouldn't she be a troublemaker, a wild one? She was a kid from the Jardín, right?

Zachary banged his head again on Bruce's arm.

39

"Cool it, kiddo." Bruce let Zachary grab his finger and suck on it. No wonder mothers looked so frazzled.

They sat down at a booth, and Bruce set down the baby seat and put Zachary in it. Bruce looked around and saw—what was his name? The football player—with two girls. One girl was beautiful—Nadine. Even he knew her name, even though he wasn't part of her group at all. He especially remembered her because when he was going with Juliana, Nadine was trying to cozy up to her. Trying to get Juliana to get her into the good parties.

Although Juliana had helped a few times, he remembered her saying, "But that's all. Either she makes it or not on her own. Besides, her brother is the Death Angel. He's connected."

The Death Angel was the leader of the Metal Jungle gang. Not someone Bruce wanted to hang around with. So what was Malena doing with Nadine?

The football player and the two girls were laughing and throwing stuff at each other. Dumb kid stuff. Things he and Juliana used to do. It still looked like fun.

"I found a great way to meet women," said Uncle Justin. He unwrapped his hamburger.

Bruce patted the baby in his carrying seat. "How's that?" he asked.

"When I'm at the store buying baby stuff for old Zach here and women find out I'm not married but helping my unmarried nephew and his baby out, they crawl all over me. A very interesting phenomenon."

"Did any of them offer to babysit?" Bruce asked, hopefully. He pulled the pickles out of his hamburger.

"No," said Uncle Justin, biting into his sandwich. "Pity."

Zachary gave a sudden cry.

"Don't worry, buddy," said Bruce. "Only the pretty ones will babysit you."

Zachary made a face like he was going to yell.

Bruce gave him his finger to suck on again. He ate one-handed.

A few minutes later, Nadine and her crew walked by. Nadine stopped and looked over at Bruce. "Hey," she said.

Uncle Justin straightened up. Bruce knew what his uncle was thinking. Wow! Get her to baby-sit!

"Hi," Bruce replied, including his hello to the other girl and the hulking football player. It was not smart to snub a football player—even in off season.

"That Juliana's kid?" asked Nadine.

"My baby," said Bruce. He'd been through this several times. It was his baby.

"What's his name?" asked the other girl.

"Zachary," Bruce said.

"Don't you run track with Malena?" asked Nadine.

"Yeah. Wasn't that her a minute ago?" he asked.

Nadine combed her hair back with her long nails. "Sure was. She's a little—" and she went into some Spanish. Bruce knew better than to ask for a translation. After she finished her tirade, Nadine stood smiling at Bruce a little. He wondered why she was even paying attention to him. Her friends shifted behind her. Nadine said, "He doesn't look like Juliana. He looks like you."

Bruce didn't quite know how to respond to that. Uncle Justin munched his hamburger.

Nadine gave Bruce a lazy smile. "Juliana is a wild one; you'd better be careful of her." Bruce had a single distinct feeling: *Get me out of here.*

The other girl tugged on Nadine's arm. "Let's go, Nadine."

Nadine gave a little wave and walked off like she was a princess. Bruce guessed she *was* in a sense: Princess Nadine of Southside.

"Later, man," said Jordan, not even looking at Bruce. They walked off, pushing and giggling.

Uncle Justin gave him a long look. "Friends of yours?"

Bruce shook his head. "They've never talked to me before."

"That girl is catty. You should have asked her if she wanted a saucer of milk."

Zachary had turned his head, watching the trio retreat, still sucking on Bruce's finger. Bruce wondered what she meant about being careful of Juliana.

CHAPTER 9

Malena

THE NIGHT AIR cooled Malena's face as she ran along the dirty sidewalk through the darkness. Shame filled her, making her heavy, weighed down with the ponderous pull of gravity. She slowed.

"Where are we going?" puffed Yolanda.

Malena jumped, forgetting Yolanda was still there. "I don't—," Malena stopped. She did know. "To the river-bed."

"Malena." Yolanda planted her legs like a balky mule. "It's dark."

"Yes, that's what happens at night," said Malena nastily.

Yolanda stamped her foot. "Now wait a minute. This is me, your best friend. Don't act like that."

Malena lowered her gaze. "I'm sorry. I don't mean it."

"I know." Yolanda pushed at her glasses. They walked on with headlights of cars zipping over them. Malena tucked her arm between Yolanda's ribs and arm and they continued, holding hands, ignoring crude comments from guys in cars.

"I wish I'd thought to get a hamburger for Peewee," said Malena.

There were no more food places around here. Just run-down apartments, old gas stations, and small, dirty liquor stores.

"We better not go back to McDonald's," said Malena. They giggled.

"He can have my fries," said Yolanda. She held up her bag. "And the rest of my shake."

"You don't mind?"

"No."

Malena squeezed her hand.

The riverbed and the overpass intersected. Cars and trucks, flowing in and out of Los Angeles, roared over the Seventh Street overpass. Their heated exhaust stung Malena's nose and eyes. She and Yolanda stood at the edge of the heavy overpass while sand sifted into her shoes.

They let go of each other, and Malena ducked first under a rusty chain-link fence and started down the dirt path filled with broken glass, bits of plastic bags, and struggling weeds. How many times had she done this, climbed under the rusting fence to see Peewee? Hundreds? Thousands? As many times as there were stars.

She climbed over concrete chunks, around piles of trash dumped out of cars off the bridge. Yolanda carefully followed, holding the fries and shake. The streetlights cast weak shadows over the edges of the riverbed. Beyond the shadows, in deeper darkness, swirled the Los Angeles river.

"Peewee," Malena called into the blackness under the bridge.

This was one of his homes.

The overpass was supported by three stanchions. Malena walked beside the nearest one. During rain, Peewee was forced up and out of the riverbed along with anyone else who lived there. When the waters ran back down, everyone moved in again.

Once Malena had seen a girl, not much older than herself, walking along the riverbed, carefully holding a plastic bag filled with fresh water.

Malena's foot rolled over a can. She grabbed at a dry, crackling bush, the leaves filthy.

A siren screamed. The angry red lights blitzed the overpass.

Malena jumped and backed into Yolanda. She called again.

No answer.

"Maybe he's not here tonight," said Yolanda.

He could be anywhere. Peewee roamed the city.

The sirens faded and stopped. Malena lifted her head. The wind was cool and scented with sage. The red cop lights slashed at the darkness across the river. A helicopter thrummed. *Time to get out of here,* she thought.

She turned to leave when a scraping sound grated over cement.

"Who?" came the voice from under the bridge.

"Peewee," Malena called, "it's me and Yolanda."

A flashlight snapped on, burning Malena's eyes. The tight gleam darted around like a bat gone mad, swooping along the cement walls of Peewee's—well, what else would you call it?—home. An old split mattress lay along the girders.

A person slumped on the mattress.

"Hey, girls," said Peewee. "Duck under here."

They did, away from the flashing lights. The whine of the helicopter remained.

Malena touched Peewee's arm. "Who is that?" She pointed toward the mattress.

Peewee shrugged. The flashlight moved up and down. "Just another one. I carried him back here. He was over on Seventh and West."

"But who loves him?" asked Yolanda softly, repeating Peewee's constant refrain that he'd asked the girls so many times.

"God does," said Malena automatically. God loved Nadine, too, didn't he? *That makes me a horrible Christian, then, because I hate Nadine.* She hated her a lot in fact.

"Sit down," said Peewee. "I haven't seen you two in a while."

Yolanda sat gingerly on a chunk of cement across from Peewee, and Malena sat next to Peewee on the edge of the piling. The unconscious guy on the mattress said something, but it made no sense. The cement chilled her rear end. She wished she had something to sit on, even a piece of cardboard to hold back the cold.

Peewee snapped off the flashlight, and they sat quietly in the dark. A bat called shrilly and the ceaseless line of traffic roared over them. The helicopter thrummed away.

As her eyes adjusted, Malena found she could see rather well, actually. The cloud cover overhead reflected the city lights back down. A large rat walked down to the river and lapped the water. The river rippled by, stumbling over trash, cheerfully brisk on its way to the ocean twenty miles away.

The stoned guy turned over, groaning. Peewee pulled a jacket up higher on the guy, then hugged his knees to his chest, rocking slowly back and forth in his thin shirt, his arms bare. Malena shivered, and she had on a shirt and a sweatshirt.

"Here," said Yolanda. "For you, Peewee." She held out the bag of fries and the melted shake.

"Ah, my favorites," Peewee said. His voice smiled. Peewee finished the fries and folded the McDonald's bag carefully and tucked it in a dark crevice.

"*Gracias*, girls," he said. His voice was stronger, like the food really did help him. He rocked again, back on his tailbone, then forward onto his toes and back again. Back and forth, back and forth.

"*De nada*," said Yolanda. Malena wished she had brought him more food. She needed to remember to do so more often.

Peewee again checked on the stoned guy. Malena knew deep inside her that she'd never be that giving, that loving to an awful person like the guy on the mattress. Someone who smelled bad, looked worse, and was so far gone that she wondered if he had any brain cells left that weren't fried. She was pained, knowing that about herself.

"Look," said Yolanda softly.

Malena lifted her head. A cluster of five guys crossed the river, splashing through the water. A couple kept looking back at the flashing lights. They strode through the deep sand, not seeing or looking under the bridge, heading across the river. They all wore dark pants and white teeshirts covered with leather jackets. Even without obvious gang wear, Malena knew who they were: Metal Jungle.

Even Peewee held his peace, not calling out a greeting like he normally would. "Not good," he murmured. Malena shot him a worried look.

The helicopter's brilliant searchlight rained down onto the riverbed. The five hurried, sand spurting under their expensive tennis shoes. Then they ran up the other side of the riverbed. Malena was glad they were gone.

Even though she'd known Nadine since fourth grade, she'd only seen Nadine's brother a couple times—once at a Christmas dinner when all the family had gathered. He was as handsome as Nadine was pretty. Malena didn't even know his real name, but everyone called him Angel, the Death Angel.

The helicopter rode the currents up and down the riverbed. The flashing lights stopped and the other side of the river grew dark, split only by the helicopter's searchlight.

"So, what's up?" asked Peewee.

Yolanda started in about Nadine and Annie and how their friendship was down the toilet.

Tears threatened to come to Malena's eyes. *I'm such a baby.* She hated herself for being so weak. Especially when obviously more serious things were happening around them. Yet she wondered, *Shouldn't friendships be held high, too?*

Peewee listened, still rocking slowly, like in films Malena had seen of people in insane asylums.

When Yolanda finished, Peewee paused as if waiting for Malena's side. She didn't have anything to add so looked out into the night, her nostrils flaring at the damp scent of the river and its decaying debris. Besides, she often felt Peewee knew things without being told. She knew he'd understand without any words from her. He was like that.

"It's okay to go different ways," said Peewee. "You can't make someone stay on your path if they don't want to. But it's wrong to make them suffer for it."

"That's what they're doing to us," said Yolanda.

Malena kept staring out into the night. Sometimes she thought she could see the battle of good against evil happening right in the riverbed with Peewee leading the charges against evil.

Peewee leaned close to Malena. She could smell the chocolate shake on his breath. "Are you doing the same back to them?" he asked.

Yolanda sputtered and pushed her glasses up higher, the light catching them in silver circles. "No way," Yolanda began. "I mean, they started it."

We are, thought Malena. *And I humiliated Nadine tonight, even though she totally deserved it.* Malena swallowed hard.

The cold wind knifed under the bridge and stabbed them. Malena hugged herself tighter. A distant church bonged the hour, nine times, the tones ringing out over the traffic and the screech of AmTrak crossing the trestle.

"My mom's gonna kill me for being out so late," said Yolanda, getting up.

Papa would be frothing at the mouth, thought Malena, but she still didn't get up.

The stoned guy moaned something in dark Spanish tones, and Peewee glanced over at him. Then satisfied he was all right, he turned back to Malena. "You're very quiet," he said, touching her shoulder.

"I'm tired. It's been a long day." An endless day.

"Win any races?"

"Last week. Against Baldwin Park High."

"Good for you."

But she had lost a more important race today.

Yolanda waited for her, shifting impatiently just out from under the bridge.

Malena moved off the cement shelf, started out, then stopped. She pulled off her sweatshirt. It should fit. He was as thin as a child. The sweatshirt wasn't new, but Mama would still be mad that she'd lost a good sweatshirt. But that was the way it had to be.

"Here." Malena thrust the sweatshirt at him. He took it soundlessly and pulled it over his head.

"It's still warm from you," he said.

Malena stepped out into the force of the night wind, her teeth chattering. Her shirt did nothing to stop the cold. Yolanda put her arm around her, and they walked out of the riverbed and hurried home through the night.

Malena wondered what the stoned guy dreamed about under the bridge. Then she knew. He didn't dream. And that was true darkness.

CHAPTER 10

Bruce

HE WAS DREAMING AGAIN about his parents.

Bruce, his parents, and Zachary had gone on a cruise to Alaska. (He knew it was a dream because there was no way his parents would go anywhere with the baby.) But the ship had gotten lost, and they were sailing among the ice floes in the Arctic, crashing into as many as they missed. The ship was slowly sinking.

His family seemed to be the only passengers aboard. He was holding Zachary, who was crying nonstop, like he did when he had colic.

His parents kept telling him, "Throw the baby overboard. It'll appease the god of the sea."

He clutched Zachary tighter. The baby's cries deafened him. "Never," he said.

"Then you're responsible for this ship sinking," said his father. His mother nodded.

Bruce hugged the baby tighter as the ship trembled under them. He trembled under the accusing stares of his parents.

Bruce suddenly woke in the dark of his room.

But the trembling continued beneath him.

He flew out of bed and grabbed the sleeping baby out of his crib. Books crashed out of the bookshelves, and Uncle Justin's old plaster models of teeth chattered to the floor.

"Bruce, Bruce," his uncle's voice rang out from the hallway. "Get up. It's an earthquake."

Holding the baby, Bruce hurried under the door frame with Uncle Justin as the shaking subsided.

Zachary began to whimper. The earth held still again. Uncle Justin grasped Bruce's shoulder. "Are you okay?" The overhead lights flicked on, and Bruce cringed at the brightness, then nearly laughed.

Uncle Justin stood in his boxer shorts, his hair standing on end.

"I'm fine," Bruce said. "Some quake, huh?"

"I guess." Uncle Justin yawned.

The baby wailed.

"Hush, hush," said Bruce softly. He took Zachary out into the hall where the light was gentle and walked up and down the hall with him. Each time Bruce passed by his room, he saw Uncle Justin picking up the fallen books and sets of teeth, placing them back on the shelves as the radio news reported the quake in low, serious tones.

Bruce went to the kitchen to fix a bottle. Zachary cried on his shoulder. He should have left the baby in his crib. Zachary would have slept through the earthquake, except—what if it had been the Big One that everyone talked about? After the '89 San Francisco-area quake, it was supposed to be just a matter of time until a quake flattened Southern California. He stared at the screaming baby. No, it was worth waking Zachary up.

When Bruce came back to his room, the overhead light was off. Only the nightlight glowed, and all the fallen junk had been picked up. Nice of him. He didn't have to do that. Uncle Justin's bedroom door down the hall was shut. The radio was still going softly. "Looks to be a 4.5 on the Richter scale. No reports of serious damage." Bruce was glad. He gave Zachary the bottle and laid the baby beside him on his bed. Bruce leaned against the wall, plumping the pillow behind him, and stifled a yawn. Zachary seemed wide awake, his gaze wandering around the room as he drank his bottle.

Bruce changed the radio to music and wondered if his parents were awake. His father was a light sleeper. One of the reasons he'd told Bruce that "there'd be no baby in his house." As if they lived in a tiny house with no privacy. Just an excuse. Bruce had had miniparties in his room, and his parents never knew.

When Bruce told his parents before Zachary was born that he was keeping the baby, Mom had gone pale and quiet, but Dad had become furious.

"This isn't a puppy we're talking about," his father had said, drawn up straight, his gray hair slicked back, his eyes fierce. His father, the business shark.

"I know we're talking about a baby and not a puppy," said Bruce, equally furious. "My baby."

"Stupid, stupid, stupid. If you had to make it with that girl, why didn't you use birth control?" Juliana was always "that girl."

Bruce didn't even bother to answer.

"Honey," his mom had slipped into the living room from the kitchen. "Adopt the baby out. So many couples desperately want a baby and can't have one of their own."

His mom did volunteer work at a home for unwed mothers. Bruce was amused at the irony but only briefly.

"So let them adopt someone else's baby. I want mine," he said to her, but he kept his eyes on his father.

Dad stomped out of the room, ending that conversation, but they had others, many others.

The day after Zachary was born, Juliana's mother called to tell him that he could come get the infant. Just like that. No emotion behind it that he could see. Paperwork had to be signed. So he went to the hospital, never saw Juliana, signed for the baby, named him officially, and there they were. The two of them. He had already gone through baby care classes at the hospital, and he gingerly, but properly, carried the baby the seven blocks home.

His father had a cow.

"Take that baby back," he commanded.

Bruce stood with his back straight, holding the sleeping infant. "I can't. This isn't a little puppy a person can take back."

His father's face turned red. "Take it back now."

Bruce wordlessly shook his head.

His father raised his head and said terribly, "Then get out."

His mother had started out behind him with a small cry, but one look from his father sent her back into the kitchen.

So Bruce got out.

He had walked a while until the baby woke—he was so small! Then he went to a phone booth. The city was darkening. He thought about who he could call for help. Friends from school? Guys from the team? Who else? There was no one else. Except his uncle whom he didn't see often. But he took a chance, called, and the rest was, as they say, history.

Zachary was falling asleep now, the bottle only half drained. Bruce was falling asleep, too. He made himself get up and put the baby back in his crib. Then he lowered the radio and lay down in bed. Zachary made funny snorting noises, and Bruce smiled, watching the baby in the low light through the crib slats.

He fell asleep to the music washing over him. Old Moody Blues tunes. One song, "The Question," touched him like soft fingers. "I'm looking for someone to change my life," went the refrain. *Someone has,* he thought. *Zachary has, Uncle Justin has, even Dad has in a way.* But he wondered at the deeper meaning of someone who could change his life. He sank into sleep before the song finished playing.

CHAPTER 11

Malena

THE NEXT MORNING, before first period, Malena ran lightly upstairs in the C building, a wide, ugly, tan two-story building, to the locker she shared with Nadine. She twirled the lock as kids walked past. A friend of hers cruised by. It was Rudy, the one who fined her for swearing. He'd recently had four gold studs punched in his left ear and seven punched in his right.

"Hey, Rudy," she called. He steered through the stream of kids, smiling lazily, and leaned against her locker. She and Rudy were buddies, friends from elementary school. They used to play along the riverbed together. In fact they'd met Peewee together back then.

"Lena, how goes it?" asked Rudy.

"Did you feel the earthquake last night?"

He shook his head. "Snored right through it." He carefully twisted each earring. "Got to keep turning them, the lady said."

"Tell me something," said Malena. The lock released and she paused, her hand on the closed locker.

"Yes, I'm available to go out with you," he said.

"Such a comedian." She gave him a playful poke. "Didn't it hurt to get your ears pierced so many times?"

"Nah."

She made a face. "That's hard to believe."

"At first I told my friend, 'Dude, this ain't my idea of a good time.' And he said, 'Rudy, dude, you want pierced ears or not?' Since I did, I took massive drugs, you know?"

"Rudy, you said you'd never do crack again."

"I took that stuff of my sister's, what's it called? For cramps?"

Malena laughed.

"It's great stuff. Seriously."

"I'll remember that," she said.

He laughed with her.

Malena opened her locker and her laughter fled. A sheet of lined note paper lay open on the pile of books. It read:

To Whatever It May Concern:

You have exactly 24 hours to remove your garbage from my (Nadine's) locker. If you don't, your garbage will be placed where it belongs—the trash can.

Nadine & Annie

It was in Nadine's handwriting, but the signatures were both Nadine's and Annie's. From the note the faint scent of Nadine's flavored lip gloss, cherry, lingered.

Malena swallowed and looked up at Rudy. *You will not cry,* she instructed herself.

"What's this?" he asked. "A death threat?"

"Almost."

He read the note over her shoulder, his breath warming her cheek. "That Nadine," he said. "She's beautiful, but it only goes so far, you know?"

She knew.

"So what are you going to do?" he asked.

"Take my stuff out. It *is* her locker. What can I say?" Malena's locker was across the junior-senior park in the B building, where she never had classes. That was why Nadine had invited her to use her locker. But that was when they were friends.

Calmly, Malena took out all her books, notebook, the mirror taped to the inside of the door, the cigar box of supplies, pencils, pens, batteries for her calculator, cough drops, sticks of gum, eyeliner, tampons, loose change. She balanced the box on top of all her books.

The warning bell jangled. Three minutes until first period.

"Let me help," said Rudy. But the cigar box began to slide off.

Malena grabbed for it and missed.

"Whoa," said Rudy, missing the box, too.

The box hit the scuffed hall floor. "Damn," said Malena. Her batteries and tampons rolled over the cracked linoleum. Her face heated up. She reached for the tampons, but Rudy got them first. He tossed them back in the box and grinned at her.

"You owe me fifty cents."

She ignored him and said, "You'll be late to class. "Go on."

"Nah, we'll hurry." They redistributed things between them and headed downstairs, moving against the rush of kids going up to first period classes.

In the B building she couldn't even remember which locker was hers. She sat on the floor and looked through her notebook. Months ago when school had started, she'd written the locker number and combination some-where in her notebook.

The halls emptied and quieted. Through a few open doors, kids glanced curiously at them. Malena's watch read forty-five seconds until the bell. Rudy didn't budge and held half of her stuff.

"This is cool," he said. "I've been late three times this week. Maybe I'll get suspended."

There! She found the locker and combination numbers written tidily on the first page of her notebook. Her locker was on the top row at the end of the hall. She stood on tiptoes and wrenched it open. They threw her garbage, as Nadine so nastily put it, inside and slammed it shut. They ran.

The late bell rang.

"Damn," said Malena.

"That's the second time," said Rudy. "Pay up." He was grinning as they raced down the halls. "You owe me a dollar."

"At lunch," she said.

"Can I trust you for it?"

She glared at him, but he just laughed.

Rudy hurried up the stairs of the C building, and she ran down the hall on the first floor for history. Ms. Reyes would mark her off. She swore again under her breath, glad Rudy didn't hear—otherwise, she'd owe him a for-tune. She skidded into class like a car out of control and slammed into her seat.

A couple kids snickered. "Home run," said one guy.

"Ms. Castillo," said Ms. Reyes, "did you know you were late?"

No kidding.

"That's a two-page paper due Friday."

Malena grimaced.

Her fourth paper since January. She used to be late more often, but Ms. Reyes was curing her. This time it wasn't quite her fault, but she had a feeling Ms. Reyes wouldn't agree. She found her notes for history.

Then as Ms. Reyes took roll, she checked in her purse to be sure she had enough money to pay Rudy. She did as long as she had a cheap lunch.

Rudy had taken it upon himself to clean up her language. "You're a Christian now. Talk like one," he told her.

The fines were a sliding scale. Fifty cents for the lesser swear words, on up to two dollars for the big-time words. She sighed and figured that if Rudy could quit drugs, then she could certainly quit swearing.

She realized she was still clutching the hateful note. She read it again, feeling herself grow warm and angry. How dare Nadine. She turned the paper over and began listing how to retaliate:

- Super-glue Nadine's lock shut
- Put dog doo doo in her locker
  (Rudy would be proud of her word choice.)
- Booby trap it so when it's opened, something flies out and hits her or spills on her.

Malena wrote down schemes all period, not listening to Ms. Reyes and her fascinating lecture on colonial America.

CHAPTER 12

Bruce

WORKOUT HAD BEEN LIGHT because of the meet the next day. Bruce stretched out and sensed someone behind him. He straightened his back and turned. Malena stood there, barefoot, like always after practice.

"Why are you barefoot?" he asked.

She looked startled. "Running shoes are expensive. I save them whenever I can."

Of course. Kids from Jardín had no money. He was lucky. His parents had money, and Uncle Justin made big bucks as a dentist. "Do you have a brother?" asked Bruce suddenly.

She looked surprised again, and he felt perversely pleased for startling her twice in a row. She'd always seemed so unflappable.

"Yeah, I got a brother. Why?"

"What if he had a baby, like I do. Would he be able to keep it?"

Malena burst out laughing.

That bugged Bruce. Zachary wasn't funny. "Never mind," he muttered, feeling like a fool for even trying to explain things. He got up.

"No, wait." She grabbed his elbow. "I wasn't laughing at you. My brother. He's only eleven and I can't imagine. . . ." Her voice trailed off, and she shrugged with a smile. "You know."

He knew. He still had trouble imaging that he had a baby. He wanted to ask her a million questions, like what she thought of him keeping the baby. Did she think he was a jerk, like most of the kids seemed to think? Like it was solely his fault that Juliana had gotten pregnant?

"I think my father would kill my brother." She let his arm loose. "My family is—you know—strict. But him keep the baby? That is a new thought," she said. "I never heard of a boy doing that, except in movies or television. In Jardín, I don't think so. The girl would, but not the boy."

He nodded, wondering how different he was than a guy from the Gardens. Of course, white guys probably wouldn't keep their kids, either. In fact the opposite happened. He knew a couple of guys who said good-bye the second their girlfriends said those magic words: I'm pregnant.

Malena swung her shoes by the laces, not quite looking at him. "I think you're *loco* for keeping a baby."

Bruce flushed angrily. Why was everyone so against it? He could tell even Uncle Justin thought he was slightly nuts for keeping Zachary.

"But," Malena held still for a moment, "for some strange reason, I admire that you have."

His anger dropped away, like a runner sprinting past a tired competitor. "Thanks," he said. "I think you're about the only one."

"Oh, no," she said as they began walking across the field. "There are others."

He wondered who they were but didn't ask.

Coach Wu hollered after them, "Bus leaves tomorrow right after fifth period. No falling down, Evans!"

"He never quits," said Bruce. At least he knew that Coach cared about his runners.

They waved at the coach and walked on, past where Malena had called to him the other day.

"Any falling down lately?" she repeated, laughter sprinkled over her words.

"Well, the earthquake almost knocked me out of bed. Does that count?"

"I know," she said, sobering. "My little sister was so scared. I had to drag her under the door frame. I was pretty scared, too."

"I didn't even get the baby and me under the door frame before it stopped." He wondered at them both taking care of kids last night. Being an only child, he never had to watch little kids. But maybe lots of kids act like parents.

The wind rustled around trees and bent grass blades on the lawns.

Bruce remembered that when he was little, he wanted to fly. He used to jump off the brick retaining wall around his house, flapping his arms and legs, trying to fly. It had always seemed to him that if he tried hard enough and the winds blew just so, he would actually fly. Instead, now he would run, the earth's equivalent of flying.

"Why did you keep the kid?" Malena asked as they crossed Walnut Ave. "You didn't have to, did you? I mean, nobody forced you, did they?"

"Not quite. In fact, when my parents kicked me out, my uncle took us in." Memories of that moment, standing in the phone booth with the whimpering newborn in his arms, hoping Uncle Justin would help and not knowing what to do if he refused, pierced him.

"That's amazingly nice of him," she said. "Why did he do that?"

"He is a great guy." After Bruce had called from the phone booth, Uncle Justin had driven over and picked them up, like he'd been waiting for Bruce's call. Uncle Justin bought all the baby equipment and paid for Nina's babysitting fees. Bruce thought his mom might be giving money to Uncle Justin, but he wasn't positive.

As to the whys, he just didn't know. There was the rivalry between Uncle Justin and Dad. Was that the only reason? He hoped not.

"You still didn't say why you kept him," she said. The wind tangled her hair around her face.

Bruce stared at the sidewalk. "I guess it was because I didn't want to run away this time. Like my parents run away from issues, from problems, like they did with Zachary. I just didn't want to be that way any more."

"I can understand that," she said. "It's too easy to bail out."

"Exactly," he said, amazed someone was understanding or at least appreciating what he was trying to do.

Behind them a car slowed. Bruce's neck hairs bristled, recognizing the Camaro engine. Juliana drove up alongside them, the tires squealing against the curb.

"Well, well," she called out the passenger window. Her voice cut the edges of her words. Then in a softer tone, she asked, "Bruce, how are you?"

Malena, standing beside him, watched with dark eyes.

"Hi, Juliana," he said, unsure how to behave, feeling caught. *That's stupid,* he told himself. *Malena and I are friends, nothing more. Juliana's the one with the new boyfriend. Why isn't she embarrassed?*

"I want to talk to you, Bruce," she called. "Let me give you a ride?" She was obviously ignoring Malena, like Malena was merely a fallen leaf.

"No, thanks," he said.

"But we gotta talk," she said. "Come on."

Now he felt like running away. Was that bailing? "Talk about what?" he asked.

"Us. The baby." She looked plaintive, her eyes wide, pleading.

He hated himself for falling prey, for wanting to see her again. But he could talk to her another time. Right now he was with a friend. "Later," he said. "I'll call you, okay?" But he didn't think he would. If she wanted to talk to him, she could make the moves.

"Bruce, now," Juliana insisted. The engine throatily accelerated, then slowed to a purr.

"No." He surprised himself with the hard edge to his words. "I'm walking Malena home."

Juliana curled her upper lip. "Soon then." She gave Malena a dagger look, something she was quite good at. The Camaro roared off.

"Arctic blast time, no?" said Malena.

He remembered his Alaskan cruise dream. He knew Juliana would say with his parents, "Throw the baby overboard."

There was an awkward pause, then Malena said, "You don't have to walk me home, Bruce. It's out of your way."

"No, I mean it. I'll walk you home."

She tossed back her long hair. "Okay, but don't be too shocked at seeing the barrio."

"I won't," he said. "I used to hang out with Luis Gomez. He lived on Fourth and Cypress. Do you know him?"

She nodded. "He's a good guy. You still see him?"

Bruce shook his head. "I don't see many people since Zachary was born."

He glanced over at her profile. Brown curves of her face outlined by black hair. She turned, catching his gaze. He turned away, flushing.

"Can I be nosy?" she asked.

He shrugged. "Sure. I guess."

"Don't see Juliana alone."

He was amused. "Don't worry. Things are over between us."

She looked angry. "No, I mean, that girl is out for blood. Don't see her alone."

Bruce started to protest. He remembered Nadine's warning about Juliana.

Malena stopped and faced him, forcing him to halt on the sidewalk. "I mean it, Bruce. Promise me that if you go talk to her, you'll at least tell someone when you go."

She was so intense, her gaze spearing him in place. Finally, he said, "Okay," just so she'd back off. Were all girls so unpredictable?

"Remember," she said as if she guessed what he was thinking. "You promised." She got out of his way, and they walked on.

The city changed. Or maybe reverted back. Perhaps where he lived, the tidy tracts, the fresh lawns, were only an illusion and not real life.

Apartment buildings clung to the sky. Paint peeled off houses. Little brown kids ran around on the sidewalks sprinkled with broken glass. Kids on bikes jetted by. Over streets littered with trash, cars rumbled, radios booming, the bass vibrating the air.

Graffiti bristled on brick walls, trash bins, any flat surface. Gang names were everywhere. Last night at McDonald's he didn't think Malena looked like the brilliant track star. She looked like she belonged here in the barrio.

He kicked a can off the sidewalk. "Can I nosy question?"

Malena tipped her head. "Fair enough."

"I saw you last night," he said.

She lifted her chin. "That's right. You and your baby were there. The baby's cute. Was that your uncle with you?"

"Yeah, that was him." He wasn't sure how to ask her, except to just ask. "Were you in a fight last night? We heard the scream and the manager yelling."

She gave him a grim smile. "We're baring our deep, dark secrets, no?"

He caught his breath. "Are you in a gang, Malena?"

She burst out laughing. Then she suddenly sat down on some broken cement steps, stopped laughing, and put her head on her knees, hiding her face. He thought she was crying.

"Malena." He touched her head. Her hair was soft. He glanced nervously around, hoping none of the homeboys would see him as the enemy and come to her rescue.

He sat beside her. Her shoulders shook. He wondered what would make her cry like that. Malena, who could run fifteen miles and make it look easy when he knew she had to be hurting. Malena, who tore a thigh muscle last year and didn't even cry then.

The wind blew over them, cool, light, He closed his eyes for a moment, suddenly weary.

When he glanced at her again, she was staring with dry eyes across the street. Two guys were walking by in baggy pants, white tee shirts, hair nets, the whole thing. Bruce began to feel acutely that he did not belong here.

Malena very slowly put her arm around his shoulders. "Lay your head on my shoulder, okay? I don't want the homeboys to get a good look at you."

He did as she told him, pressed his face into her small shoulder, and closed his eyes. She leaned over his face, her long hair a curtain hiding him. She smelled of heat and soap. Her hair smelled of some kind of flowers. When he opened his eyes, he could see the pulse in her throat.

A long moment went by, and then she said, "They have gone." He didn't move, and she gave him a slight push.

Bruce sat up, his face warm. "Who—"

"Metal Jungle. It's better if they don't see you," she said.

He wanted to ask her more about the Metal Jungle, about the barrio, about her life, but he asked, "Were you crying?"

She shook her head. "I think I'm past crying." She gave him a wan smile. "You'd think I'd broken up with my boyfriend or something. Isn't that supposed to be the worst pain for high school kids?"

He didn't answer but clenched his hands together so he wouldn't take her in his arms.

"But for me it's not a guy," she said. "It's my best friends. Only they aren't my best friends anymore. The thing in McDonald's was the final breakup."

"Why did you break up?" he asked.

"This I don't know." She picked at the crumbling cement. "We've known each other since fourth grade."

"That's a long time." He hadn't had friends like that. Most of his friends were guys he played ball with or ran with. Nothing more.

The door behind them opened, and a woman's voice, shrill and incessant, in words he didn't understand— why had he taken German instead of Spanish?—startled them to their feet. Malena spoke to the woman in soothing Spanish. The woman, her face full of wrinkles, quieted. But Bruce was glad when he and Malena walked on.

Two little girls with hair in braids to their skinny waists ran up the street toward them. "Malena!" one cried. "Play hopscotch with us?"

"In a while," she said. "Go ask Lucia to play, okay? I'll be there in a little while."

One with a small, oval face scowled at Bruce. She looked like a gnome. A city gnome. He smiled, but she stamped her foot and stuck her tongue out at him. Then the little girls ran off.

Bruce was taken aback. "Well," he said. "I guess she told me."

"Ah, Rosa. If something doesn't go her way, well, she has to find someone to blame."

Malena gave him an apologetic smile. Suddenly, she grabbed his arm and half turned him. "Don't look," she said.

His heart pounded in fear, sure the Metal Jungle would fall on him this time.

"Make a wish," she said. "The first star is out this evening. Close your eyes and make a wish."

He closed his eyes. "I wish . . . ," he began.

"Not out loud! Or it doesn't work."

He wished suddenly and deeply that he and Malena would be friends.

Real friends.

CHAPTER 13

Malena

"HE WALKED YOU HOME?" asked Yolanda that evening.

"It's not like you think," said Malena. "We're just getting to be friends."

They lay on their backs on Malena's bed. Lucia tapped her feet to the radio, pretending to do homework, but Malena knew her sister was spying on them.

"You know that love begins with friendship," said Yolanda.

Malena smiled. Then she took Yolanda's arm and they got up.

"Where are you going?" called Lucia.

Malena said, "Out," and shut the bedroom door behind them.

Thwarted, Lucia bellowed from behind the closed door, but Malena hurried Yolanda outside.

They sat on the small front porch on a wooden crate that Papa had brought home from work.

The sky held no stars now. The smog and fog had mixed together in a gray, dingy mess and ruined the sky. She hoped Bruce really had wished on that star because she'd given up her wish. Only one person per star. There were so few times when there were stars to even wish on.

Some astronomer she made. Not very scientific. She sighed deeply.

"So what happened?" asked Yolanda.

"What do you mean?"

"With you and Bruce?"

"Nothing. He walked me here." She pointed at some dirt in front of the porch. "And he walked back down the sidewalk, and I went in the house."

Yolanda sighed. "It's wonderful. Like a date, maybe?"

"Maybe," said Malena doubtfully. It hadn't felt like a date, but then what did a date feel like? She hardly knew.

"Yet he did get what's-her-name in trouble."

Malena rubbed her nose. "So do lots of guys. And none of them keep their babies."

"That is weird, isn't it?"

"Yeah. But I like him for it."

They talked a while longer about guys and getting married.

"I doubt I will get married," said Yolanda. "I'm sure I'll have a brief, tragic life."

Malena laughed. "You should be an actress."

Yolanda looked pleased. "Think so?"

"Why not? Dream big."

"That's hard to do here, isn't it?"

Malena looked up at the shrouded sky. "Yeah."

Papa called to Malena through the window. "Inside, *mi hija.*" Inside, my daughter.

"Okay." But Malena didn't get up. She turned to Yolanda. "I have an idea how to get back at Nadine."

Yolanda's eyes gleamed. "Oh, Malena, you shouldn't. What is it?"

"I'll show you tomorrow, okay?"

"Malena!" Papa again.

Yolanda jumped up. "See you tomorrow, Lena."

Malena went back inside. Papa glowered at her.

"Papa, I'm having hard times," she said. "I was talking it over with Yolanda."

He softened. "What's the matter?"

"Nadine."

"She's not worth it," he said, crossing his arms over his chest. It was all Malena could do not to throw herself at him and be his little girl again.

"But I once loved her, Papa."

He locked the front door. "No, Malena. I think not. Love does not go away."

She wondered at that. Would she want revenge on Nadine if she really loved her? What about Juliana? That girl wanted revenge if anybody did. Malena could practically smell it. But Juliana had once loved Bruce, hadn't she? Malena remembered a party they'd been at last year. Juliana was walking around telling people she was in love. She was also stoned. But still, what happened to her love? Hadn't Bruce once loved her? Malena could tell he was torn.

It was all so complicated.

She finished her homework. Lucia was asleep, the radio blaring in her ear. Malena turned it off and climbed into bed. Later, in the deep night, she woke suddenly, heart hammering, thinking she felt another earthquake but realizing it was only herself shaking. She was dreaming that she wasn't a whole number anymore.

CHAPTER 14

Bruce

AT LUNCH the following day Bruce sat by himself, as usual, in the corner at the end of one of the long tables and began eating what the school cafeteria called "Beef Surprise." Yeah, a real surprise because no one knew what it was, or worse, they knew but wouldn't tell.

When he'd dropped Zachary off at Nina's this morning, Zachary had been whining, clinging to him. He wished he could stay with the baby.

"Sorry, kiddo," he said, handing him over to Nina. Zachary wailed, his face red, contorted, snot running down over his wailing mouth. Completely gross, but Bruce wanted to hold him, comfort him.

Nina just smiled with the baby yelling on her shoulder. "Go on to school. He'll settle down." So Bruce had left.

Maybe now he should call Nina and see how the baby was doing. He didn't want to bug Nina, though, and the ringing phone might wake up the babies.

He mechanically ate his food, looking around, feeling like he was the only person who sat alone. Out through the wide open doors of the cafeteria, he could see across the park. Malena was eating with the thin, tall girl with glasses he'd seen her with at McDonald's.

A guy he'd seen hanging around her before was with them. Her boyfriend? Or the other girl's boyfriend?

Matt from track appeared beside him. "Old buddy, how goes it?"

Bruce gave him a punch. "Okay." He didn't want to dump on Matt.

"Haven't seen you much," said Matt bouncing on his heels.

"Yeah, well, you know how it is. I'm a busy single parent."

Matt grinned, his sandy hair in his eyes. "Come on, eat with us. Don't be such an old woman." He led Bruce over to some other members of the track team, and they greeted him in a friendly way. Bruce relaxed, feeling like he belonged, at least for lunch period.

CHAPTER 15

Malena

MALENA FOLDED her paper bag and put it in her note-book to use again for tomorrow's lunch.

Rudy uncrossed his legs. "See you guys. Gonna go talk to some dudes." He ambled off.

"He's nice," said Yolanda, pushing up her glasses.

Malena nodded, not paying attention. Her gaze fixed on Jordan, approaching alone, carrying a tray from the burger bar. Nadine sat across the park, her head up, waiting for Jordan.

Now was the time to act.

"Hey, Jordan," Malena called.

He turned slowly, like a Miss America, totally used to attention. Or maybe more like a show dog. Malena grinned deep inside of her, but it wasn't a pleasant grin, more like a grimace of pain.

"Yeah?" Jordan stood over her. "How's it going, wild one?"

"Have a seat," said Malena, patting the grass. She sat up straighter, tucking her bare legs under her skirt. Jordan sprawled on the grass beside them. Without even looking back to Nadine! Malena wanted to kick him.

"You're awesome on the track," said Jordan. "I might add, off the track, too."

Yolanda strangled on her sandwich. Jordan glanced at her curiously and took a bite of his burger.

"Thanks," said Malena. "So, like, I don't know much about you, but I want to." Her lie made her want to gag, but she went on. "What do you want to do after school?"

He looked puzzled. "I'll work out today. Weights."

Imbecile. "No, I mean when you graduate."

"Oh. Play football."

"Professionally?"

"Sure. Whatever."

Why was she doing this to herself? She grimly went on. "What else do you like?"

He took another bite of burger. "What do you mean?"

"Like what things do you do, Jordan? You know, hobbies."

He grinned and wiped his mouth with the back of his hand. "Oh, I like to party, and I like to drink beer and go out with girls." He winked at her.

She wanted to throw up.

Yolanda made another strangled sound and went off in search of the drinking fountain. Jordan gave her a raised-eyebrow look.

"Don't mind her," said Malena. "She's shy around guys."

"Oh, yeah," he said knowingly. "She's not bad looking, though. Tell her to get rid of the glasses."

"What does that mean?" she snapped, regretting it instantly. Jordan's mouth drooped. "I only meant that she should dress more in style, you know," he said. "Guys like girls without glasses."

She bit back her retorts and knew she'd owe the national debt to Rudy if her thoughts were rung up. "Yolanda is my friend," said Malena stubbornly. "Don't insult her."

"I didn't mean to. I know you and her are tight." Then he went on to tell her his image of a good-looking girl, which suspiciously sounded like herself.

Out of the corner of her eye she caught Nadine walking toward them. Jordan had his back to Nadine. Time collided.

"So do I fit your image?" Malena asked, leaning close to him.

His scent of after-shave gagged her, but she forced herself not to recoil.

"Well, you'll do." He grinned.

Her palm itched to slap him. "You know," she said, trying to look dreamily into his eyes. "Would you mind, I mean, I'd love it if you'd kiss me."

His eyes popped. "Aww-right." He grabbed her and kissed her long and hard. Onions on his breath from his burger revulsed her. Talk about toxic waste. She made herself relax, not straight-arm him or kick him where it counted.

"Well, Jordan. Lowering yourself?" Nadine's voice split air molecules. Jordan sprang back as if Malena had bitten him.

She wished she had.

He looked stunned, staring up at Nadine as if to explain but not seeming to know what had even happened. A sick feeling spilled into Malena's stomach.

Malena got up, holding her notebook in front of her like a shield. She knew she would be in for some heavy repenting. "Oh, Nadine, I got your note. No wonder Jordan is looking elsewhere."

Nadine turned as white as her short skirt. "What's with kissing her, Jordan?" she demanded.

"Yeah, Jordan, you two-timer," said Malena.

"I was just—" He broke off.

"Just what?" demanded Nadine.

Yolanda materialized beside Malena and whispered, "What have you done?"

"You can keep him," Malena told Nadine. "You two deserve each other." She grabbed Yolanda's arm, and they marched off.

Jordan's voice swept over to them, explaining. "She asked me to kiss her."

"Oh, and you just had to?"

Malena and Yolanda fled into the center of the park among the cluster of eucalyptus trees.

"Malena," said Yolanda. "I saw you kiss him. That was the revenge?"

Malena looked at her friend. "Yeah, pretty sick, no?" They walked past a bench of guys and one of them was Bruce. He stared at her, shocked. Why did he always show up when she was at her worst? Her shoulders sagged, and she wanted to take back all she had done.

CHAPTER 16

Bruce

THE BELL BLARED, ending second lunch. Bruce tossed his cardboard tray into the trash. Malena and her friend walked off. As nice as she'd been to him, she still was an unknown mixture. He remembered his chemistry midterm, where they had to identify various compounds. In this case, Malena was an element he wasn't familiar with.

But did anyone really know a friend completely? He hardly knew himself, let alone another person.

"Earth to Bruce," said Matt, elbowing him.

"Pops," said Dan, the javelin thrower. "Wake up."

Bruce blinked. "What?"

"I said, 'What's with you and Castillo?' " Dan was grinning.

"What do you mean?" asked Bruce. He drained his milk.

"You know. Speedy Gonzalez herself. You guys hanging out together all of a sudden?"

"We're just talking. Is that a crime?" *Be cool,* Bruce told himself. *They're teasing you. Don't be so uptight.*

"You tell me," said Dan, laughing like a coyote. "I'm not the one with a kid."

Bruce threw his empty milk carton at him. "Get out of town."

Dan laughed. He packed muscles and could bench press twice what Bruce could. Bruce didn't want to get him really mad. He knew Dan was just trying to push it to the limit.

"Okay, leave him alone," Matt told Dan. Then to Bruce he said, "Dan's only jealous. He never even gets a second date from a girl."

"That ain't true," said Dan as the bell rang. "I went out with Diane McMillan four times."

"Set a record, dude," said Matt. "Hey Bruce, how many times did you go out with Juliana before she gave in?"

The conversation was turning in a direction he didn't want to go. "Later, okay?"

"Tell us your secret," said Matt. "Dan needs to know."

Bruce left them punching each other and laughing. Running upstairs to his locker, his brain answered the question: only three dates. He could hear his dad's voice: "Third time's a charm." In this case it was.

He had thought Juliana was really hot for him. But now he decided she had been just looking to score. Everyone said it was just guys who wanted to score. But no, some girls did, too.

She had acted real cool, sophisticated, like going to bed with someone was nothing. But later as he thought about it, he figured she was just lonely—he understood about that—and that he was a convenient way to keep those feelings away. Her parents cared about the appearance of stuff. They didn't care about her especially. Not the real her. They were mad at him for keeping the baby because that reminded people that it had been Juliana's baby, too.

He opened his locker and stood looking into it like it was a magic mirror to the past.

He remembered a conversation they'd had just after the first time they'd had sex. Not her first time. But his.

"I don't think I'll ever get married," she said, lying back, her blond hair frothing around her shoulders.

He propped his head up on his elbow, marveling at her softness, her beauty. "Why not?"

She shrugged. "There are so many people. How can you ever decide who to stay with for the rest of your life? That seems impossible to decide. Did you read that science fiction book, *Time Enough For Love?* That's what it's about. Loving different people. I'd like to stay with a guy for a few years, get to know him, then move on to someone else."

She'd said it so innocently, like she really meant it. With none of her customary toughness. *She really believed it,* he thought. But he knew it couldn't be true. He wasn't sure how you decided on one person, either, but he knew he was jealous. Some other guy having her in a few years? No way. He had wanted all of her, forever.

Bruce blinked at his locker. Forever had lasted four months.

"Hey, Bruce." The voice interrupted his thoughts.

His hand tightened on his locker door, and he turned.

Like a magical spell reworked, Juliana was leaning against the lockers, smoking one of those thin, brown cigarettes, the smoke curling up around her head. She looked like a beautiful dragon.

"Hey, Juliana." He swallowed.

"Why are you avoiding me?" She stepped closer to him.

He pulled out his notebook and his German book. "Am I?" he asked mildly, shutting the locker door. "It seems to me you're the one who told me you hated me completely and thoroughly and that you never wanted to see me again."

"Oh, that." She laughed. "I was mad because you got me pregnant. That's all."

That's all. No problem.

They stared at each other. Kids streamed by. Now she looked more like the thin, chiseled Arabian horse she used to ride. Arrogant, high-headed like her horse.

"I just thought we could, you know, get together some time soon. Catch up," she said. "I really want to see you."

He began walking toward his class. He had no idea what class Juliana had for fifth period. Last year they'd meet after each class for a fraction of a second for a quick kiss.

"I don't know when," he said. "I'm pretty busy with the baby."

She blanched a little. "Maybe I could come over some time and see it, see him."

He couldn't believe she was saying that. She'd said she never wanted to see Zachary. Ever.

He guessed his idea of ever and forever were different from hers.

They stopped at Bruce's classroom. Juliana swung her car keys under his nose. "How about tonight?"

He shook his head. That was too soon. He had to think about this. "I have a track meet and a lot of homework."

"Tomorrow," she persisted. "I'll take you home after school."

"I have track workout."

"I can wait. I used to all the time, remember?"

He remembered. He couldn't really think of a concrete reason to say no. Part of him was saying, Take a chance.

Maybe she's changed. Why shouldn't he be friends with her? She was Zachary's mother, after all. One day the kid might like to meet her.

"Okay," he said finally. "Tomorrow after workouts."

"Good." She flicked him under the chin like she used to do, then hurried down the beige school hall.

He went into his classroom, puzzled.

CHAPTER 17

Malena

THAT AFTERNOON the track meet was away, at El Monte High. Malena sat on the grass of the football field, old ridges from cleats and falling bodies under her, and the sunlight slanting down on her. While the high hurdlers ran their races, she finished her letter to Tia Kate:

I like math. I can see why you must, too. Math is so logical, orderly, neat. Everything works out. But then I was reading about quantum physics, and it turns out that things aren't so orderly. I mean, quarks, the weird subatomic parts, don't behave like scientists expect.

This is my theory. I've thought a lot about it. Well, since this morning. Arithmetic is for people who want to believe life is simple. People who are into surface stuff, superficial. But higher math is for people who want the complicated truth, the real truth.

I want that kind of truth. . . .

"Love letter?" asked Becky. The petite Vietnamese girl knelt in the grass beside Malena.

"Not quite." Malena grinned. "My aunt."

Becky stretched out on the grass, her head touching her knees.

Their skin was nearly the same shade of brown, but Becky's was more milky, and Malena's was more olive.

"One of my aunts is younger than me," Becky said. "Isn't that odd?"

"Most relatives are odd," said Malena. "Especially brothers."

Becky grinned in agreement. "I've got two. They are *very* odd."

Becky's race was called: 440 low hurdles. She trotted off to the blocks. The gun fired and the runners launched. Malena marveled that Becky, just a little over five feet, cleared the hurdles like a gazelle.

A shadow fell over her. She looked up.

"Hi," said Bruce.

She squinted. "How's it going?"

"Weird."

She sighed. "I know that feeling."

Bruce hesitated and asked, "Are you and that football guy going out?"

"Who?" Then it struck her. *Jordan.* She plucked a dandelion out of the grass and blew the seeds. They rose on the winds like miniature clouds and briskly sailed away. She laid the empty stalk down next to her. "No," she said. "Actually, I hate him."

Bruce raised his eyebrows. "You could have fooled me."

"That was the point."

He carefully retied his Nike running shoes, then just looked at her. "That doesn't make much sense."

Malena wanted to say, "I know. It doesn't make much sense to me, either," but she just put her chin in her hands and said, "See, I wanted to get back at Nadine. Jordan's her new boyfriend."

"Not a very faithful boyfriend."

Nor was she a faithful friend.

Malena picked another dandelion and blew, not offering the wish to Bruce this time. She wished for calmness and peace instead of this churning. The seeds floated up, unhurried, meandering along the breeze. She wished for faithfulness.

The hurdle races finished and kids pulled the starting blocks off the track to prepare for the long-distance races. Junior varsity was first. Then, them.

"Let's go," yelled Coach Wu. His face was shiny with sweat. "You a bunch of cattle or what? Start warming up."

Bruce ambled over to Matt and stretched with him.

Malena stretched alone. *Why don't you make everything okay, God?*

Because you totally bungled things, Malena. Why should God take the rap?

Can't you just fix stuff, God?

No, because then we'd all be robots, with no choice.

Being a robot would be easier. But she knew deep inside that she didn't really want to be a robot, a puppet like Annie was.

She touched her toes in a fluid motion and kept reaching.

Life was like a race. You didn't know for sure if you'd win, but at least if you finished, trying all the way, you'd know you'd done what you could.

She peeled off her sweats and adjusted her nylon shorts. Then she wondered, *what if Nadine and Annie suddenly changed and decided they could all be friends again, would that work?*

It would be tough. So much had already happened, like betrayal. *Would you be willing?* she asked herself. *Could you forgive them?*

Her mouth tightened. No, probably not. They had gone too far. But what's the point of forgiveness if it's easy?

She turned away to the track, watching the junior varsity boys line up. As she waited for her race, she knew she wanted to always run her best.

CHAPTER 18

Bruce

BRUCE WON the two-mile race. Guys didn't race the girls, so Malena wasn't one of his competitors. He knew that if she were, he wouldn't have been first. He wiped his face with the end of his tee shirt.

Matt punched his shoulder. "Way to go, dude!"

"Thanks. You, too." Matt had come in second. Bruce grinned at Matt. "What a team, huh?"

"There's goes Speedy Gonzalez," said Matt.

They watched the girls start. Malena moved easily, tidily, clinging to the edge of the lead the whole seven laps. Then at the final lap she kicked and took the lead to win the two-mile race. El Monte's girls straggled in after Malena was already cooling down.

Bruce went up to Malena, who was taking deep breaths, but her eyes were bright. "Good run," he said.

"Thanks. You did good, too."

Bruce felt warm, like everything was all right again.

He stood with her, watching the final race, the 440 relay. Southside dropped the baton during the second pass.

"Idiots!" Bruce yelled. He couldn't believe they dropped the baton!

Apparently Coach Wu couldn't believe it either. He was shrieking at the runners.

El Monte beat them in the relay. But overall Southside didn't do too badly.

Bruce walked back to the bus with Malena. "Two miles is nothing," she said. "Want to run with me at the dam? Get some real exercise?"

"I have to pick up Zachary," he said, trying to think how that could work. Nina was firm about him getting the baby right after track. "I do have this baby backpack thing, but I've never tried running with him."

"So try it," she said.

He thought he would. Zachary would probably like being outside.

During the bus trip home Coach Wu sang them a Chinese victory song, nasal and whining.

"He needs to be put out of his misery," said Dan.

Coach Wu sang all the way home. It was pretty bad. A singer, the man wasn't. Bruce just grinned at Malena. Coach was too much.

After they got off the bus at Southside High, they walked to Nina's to pick up the baby.

"Hi, kiddo," Bruce said softly as he put the sweater on the baby. Malena stood back, watching.

Bruce wondered what she thought about him and the kid. Then he tucked the baby in the backpack and shouldered it. They set off for the dam about fifteen minutes away. Zachary gurgled, and his wet fingers played along Bruce's neck.

"He'll be almost two when you graduate," said Malena. "Are you going to go to college with him?"

"I can hardly imagine that. I'll just be glad when he starts sleeping through the night," said Bruce. "But yeah, I want to go on to college. Maybe I'll go to Cal State, LA. Someplace close by." Would Uncle Justin still be footing the bills even then? That seemed too much to ask.

At the top of the dam, the wind snaked around them, stronger up there. They began jogging, heading down the steep hill to the sandy paths on the bottom. This part of the riverbed was usually empty of people. Or at least it was harder to see people because of the dense screens of bamboo and other bushes.

As they reached the bottom of the hill, Bruce pointed to the baby on his back. "Does he look okay?" He didn't know if Zachary would get motion sickness or what. Zachary's little fingers still clung to Bruce's hair and neck.

"He's smiling," said Malena.

"Good."

They jogged until Bruce's shoulders ached. Then they walked in the dusk. Zachary gave a whimper, his way of telling Bruce, "Uh, Dad, the bottle, please."

"I better start home," said Bruce.

"Sure," said Malena. Without him asking, she adjusted the blanket to protect Zachary's head from the cold air.

They walked back up the steep hill to the top of the dam. The streetlights came on, casting deep orange pools in the gathering fog.

"You're a pretty good mom," said Malena.

"You think so?" he asked anxiously. "What if he grows up totally warped?"

Malena laughed. "I don't think so. You care about him too much."

Bruce hoped caring would be enough.

They stopped at the corner where Malena would head for Jardín and Bruce for Uncle Justin's in the hills. Zachary burbled under his blanket, being patient, but Bruce knew he'd be screaming soon.

"My parents told me I was being selfish, keeping Zachary." Bruce shifted the pack. It felt heavy now.

"Selfish?" she said. "It sounds pretty selfless to me."

"My parents thought I was trying to get back at them or something." The wind swirled around them, dancing loose pieces of paper between them.

"Were you?"

"No. I just wanted to do something right." *For once,* he thought. *Just for once.*

"It *was* right," said Malena gently. "How could it not be?"

He could think of a few ways, but he didn't say them, and he was grateful for Malena's kindness.

They parted. Malena leaped across the street, her long braid bouncing, then she was gone in the shadows between streetlights. Bruce walked back to Uncle Justin's. Zachary alternated between gurgling and yelping from hunger.

A song flooded Bruce's mind. That old Moody Blues song trickled over him: "I'm looking for someone to change my life / I'm looking for a miracle in my life. . . ."

That's it, he thought. He had been looking for something, someone to change things for him. All along. But was that realistic? Didn't you have to do everything yourself? Wasn't that the way to do things? Besides, who could really change you? Inside that is. Could a person do that?

Zachary wailed for the last few blocks home. When Bruce finally got the bottle ready and stuck it in the baby's mouth, Zachary rolled his eyes shut in bliss.

CHAPTER 19

Malena

Malena worked on her bed, graphing trig problems. She chewed on the metal end of her pencil, the eraser long gone from many earlier mistakes.

Lucia jumped onto the foot of her bed.

"Hey," said Malena. Her pencil skiddeded across the graph paper, and the fat pink eraser bounced off the bed. "Leave me alone, Lucia." She hunted for the eraser on the floor.

"You never play with me anymore," Lucia announced.

Malena blinked and looked up. "You're right. I don't."

Tears flooded Lucia's eyes. "Why won't you?"

"Lucia, I'm fifteen years old. I'm not a kid anymore—" She broke off as a tear ran down Lucia's cheek and dripped off her chin. "Oh, Lucia, don't cry."

Malena put down her pencil.

Lucia sniffed loudly. "I'm never going to grow up," she said. "I want to keep playing. Grown-ups never play."

"I do play, but it's different than when you're a kid."

"How?" Lucia fixed her gaze on her sister.

Malena bit her lip. How did she play? "I run track. That's fun for me. I see my friends and talk and joke around. Yolanda and I have tons of fun together." Used to be Yolanda, Nadine, and Annie. Malena sighed. "I still play games and stuff. We played those marathon Monopoly games together with Carlos and Yolanda, remember? Wasn't that fun?"

Lucia gave a tiny nod, then said, "But that was last summer."

"Well, stuff that isn't fun as a kid *is* fun as a grown-up." Did she qualify as a grown-up? Her parents didn't think so. But Bruce was only a grade ahead of her and a parent. Did that make him a grown-up?

"Like what stuff?"

"Like talking to people. Really talking with them." She thought of Bruce, Peewee, Rudy, Yolanda. "And going to parties and hanging out with friends. Stuff like that." She finished lamely. Maybe kids did have more fun. But you couldn't be a kid all your life, could you?

"So," said Lucia, drawing the word out thoughtfully. "You do play but not with me."

The kid was too logical. "Have you thought about becoming a philosopher?"

"A phil-lost-what?"

"Never mind." Malena resigned herself to finishing her homework later. She picked up a ball of brownish-green clay from the card table. "I wonder if I can still make a cat?"

"Of course you can," said Lucia seriously.

They sat and made clay animals. Lucia play-talked to the animals, but Malena couldn't quite relax enough to slip into the imaginary world. She mostly smiled at Lucia's conversations. A deep longing invaded her and wouldn't go away.

93

CHAPTER 20

Bruce

NEXT MORNING.

The kitchen clock read six-fourteen. Bruce turned on the radio and flipped to the classic rock station. He put the baby in his seat while fixing the bottle.

Zachary whined and squirmed.

"You gotta wait, kiddo," he said.

When the formula was warm, he stuck the bottle in Zachary's mouth and sort of propped it up so Zachary could drink while he fixed his own breakfast. He'd read a couple of books about babies, and they all suggested holding the baby while feeding him. But they didn't explain how to do that while you were trying to do fifty other things.

He popped toast in the toaster as Uncle Justin came into the kitchen, rubbing his eyes. "Is it daylight already?"

Bruce just grinned at him.

When the slices of toast popped out, Bruce spread margarine on them. Uncle Justin got a cup of coffee and tickled Zachary's foot. The baby smiled around the bottle.

Bruce sat at the table with his toast and cold cereal. "Uncle Justin," he said suddenly, "why are you helping Zachary and me?"

His uncle sipped his coffee and tapped the kitchen counter with his fingers. "Because you needed help and your parents, especially your father, wasn't about to go to bat for you."

But why? Bruce wondered. *What makes someone do a selfless act?* "Have you and Dad *ever* gotten along?" he asked instead.

Uncle Justin chuckled. "That doesn't make us sound very friendly, does it?"

Bruce smiled at his reference to the word *friendly.* Uncle Justin liked to insist that he was a friendly dentist, and Bruce would say, "Oh, sure, just like the movie, *Little Shop of Horrors*?" Uncle Justin would do his Steve Martin imitation of the evil dentist, which always made Bruce laugh.

"Your father and I view the world very differently," said Uncle Justin.

Zachary stopped drinking a moment and stared at Uncle Justin.

"I think I try to *understand* people and situations, but George tries to *conquer* people and situations," Uncle Justin continued. "Maybe it's because we're so far apart in age. Maybe that's why we're so different. Your grandfather, my dad, was a lot like your father."

Bruce ate his toast thoughtfully. *But you're not like Grandfather,* thought Bruce. But then Grandfather Evans had died when Uncle Justin was only seven, so he didn't have as much time to influence Uncle Justin as he had Dad.

Bruce spooned up his cereal. Even though Uncle Justin was fifteen years younger than Dad, it was Dad who would act like a kid with temper bursts and lots of yelling. Just before Zachary was born, Bruce had signed paperwork stating that he was the lawful father and that he was planning to keep the baby. When he told Dad about it, Dad shouted, "What have you gotten yourself into now?"

"You knew about the baby coming," Bruce said.

"Yes, but to keep it!" Dad yelled for days about that.

Then when Uncle Justin had let Bruce and Zachary move in, Dad had turned his anger on his brother. "What do you mean, butting into this?"

Uncle Justin crossed his arms over his chest and lifted his head. "Bruce asked me for help," he said, "because you, his parents, wouldn't help." Mom was sobbing in the kitchen. Bruce wanted to go to her but didn't dare.

"Get serious, Justin," Dad said. "How is Bruce going to go to school? Do you expect him to drop out and care for an infant?"

Dad wasn't even making sense. Bruce would find a babysitter. Lots of people had their kids in childcare.

Uncle Justin was relentless. "You're making this a bigger issue that it is. Isn't it because you're embarrassed about Bruce keeping his son? About how that reflects on you?"

"I am concerned that Bruce have a chance to go to college, get a decent job. How is he going to do that with a child?" Dad shouted back.

"He won't be the first person to go to college with a young child," said Uncle Justin.

Bruce felt as if he were watching a Ping-Pong match. Back and forth. Perhaps he was the Ping-Pong ball. No one was asking him what he thought. He had considered these things. He wasn't going into this with his eyes closed. Bruce cleared his throat, and the two men stopped talking and looked at him.

"Dad," Bruce began, "I know this is going to be difficult—"

"No, it won't," said Dad in a crystal clear voice. "Because the baby won't be around to cause trouble."

"I won't give him up!" Bruce began to panic. They couldn't force him, could they? He looked frantically at Uncle Justin. He'd promised to help. Would he back down?

"Lots of couples are dying to adopt a white infant," said Dad. "Get serious, Bruce. You're sixteen years old. You have got at least six, eight more years of school to go."

Uncle Justin started to speak, and Dad whirled like a rabid dog. "You stay out of this! You've caused enough problems in this family."

No, Dad, you've caused the problems. You always have, forcing everyone to do things your way.

"Now, Bruce," said Dad, pinning him in place with his steely gaze. "Are you going to be sensible and give up that baby for adoption?"

His name is Zachary, thought Bruce, and this was the most sensible thing he'd ever done. But he also knew that there was a good chance that his father would never forgive him for not backing down. But if he did, he'd never forgive himself.

He wished Dad would change his mind. He wished he'd try to understand. He wished. . . .

But that was many months ago. "If you hadn't helped me," said Bruce as he stared at his breakfast, "I know I wouldn't have been able to keep Zachary. Thanks, really. I know it's expensive and—"

Uncle Justin waved his hand. "Don't worry about it. For once I'm helping someone and not just doing whatever I want. It's good for me."

They ate silently. Zachary, done with his bottle, dropped it to the floor and grinned unexpectantly at Bruce.

"Why does Dad get so bent out of shape when I do something other than exactly what he wants?" asked Bruce.

"What do you do when you want your own way and can't get it?" asked Uncle Justin.

"That's what it is? He just wants his own way?"

Uncle Justin sipped his coffee. "That's the way it looks to me. He likes being in charge. And maybe he actually feels so helpless inside that he has to try and run things."

Dad helpless? Bruce turned the idea over. Did he want to run lives like his father did? Was he helping or running Zachary's life? But Zachary was a little kid and needed someone to run his life, at least for a while. Maybe Dad still thought Bruce was a little kid and wanted to run his life.

Bruce felt as if he were reading a Choose Your Own Adventure book. Is Dad running my life? Turn to page 10. Or is Dad really just showing concern? Turn to page 6.

"I want to run my own life," said Bruce.

"Of course you do," said Uncle Justin. "You need to do that."

Bruce thought more about it. Uncle Justin sure wasn't running his life. Uncle Justin was helping him. Did that mean Bruce was running Uncle Justin's life? No, there was a middle ground, a balance.

"Do you feel helpless?" asked Bruce.

"Sure," said Uncle Justin. "Babies, not to mention teenagers, are new terrain for me, too."

Bruce finished his cereal, and Uncle Justin went to get dressed for work. Bruce had always thought people did things that helped others only if it helped them, too. But all Uncle Justin was getting out of this deal was a lower bank account, an awkward teenage boy, and a noisy, smelly baby.

Then there was Malena, who had waited for him, concerned about him when he fell. Was she being like Uncle Justin, or did she have some other motive? She couldn't be wanting a boyfriend or anything, could she? He wasn't a very good candidate. She must know that.

It was odd having people gather around him to help him. Usually, he'd felt he was alone, fighting to find the path on his own.

But now. . . .

He wasn't alone anymore.

CHAPTER 21

Malena

JUST OUTSIDE THE SCHOOL, Malena dug in her pocket for a cherry cough drop. Yolanda slowed beside her, swinging her purse. Sea gulls, bracketed by crows, flapped lazily across the front lawn of the school. Malena tossed up one cough drop, and a speckled, brown gull stooped and neatly swiped the drop out of the air. The other gulls chased it, and the crows cawed in frustration, but the gull had swallowed the drop instantly.

"Smart bird," said Malena as they walked across the lawn.

Yolanda sighed. "I have this big test in Spanish today. I'm so nervous."

"You'll be okay," said Malena. "You spoke Spanish before you spoke English." They walked between buildings A and C, heading for Malena's locker in the B building.

"That doesn't matter. Mr. Brandon is rough."

"What kind of name is that? Not Mexican."

"He knows five languages. He's super smart."

Malena punched Yolanda's arm lightly. "When we're out of school, I'll be an astrophysicist, and you'll be a world-famous diplomat."

Yolanda wrinkled her nose and dumped her books in Malena's locker. Malena redid her lipstick in the mirror taped on the door.

"Speaking of diplomatic," said Yolanda. "What are you going to do next?"

"About what?" But Malena knew what Yolanda was talking about. She capped her lipstick.

"Don't play dumb, Ms. Astrophysicist. What are you going to do about you-know-who?"

Malena surprised herself. "I'm not going to do anything."

"Why not? You were ready to kill."

"I know." Malena shut her locker as the warning bell shrilled. Together they climbed the stairs of the C building and stood outside Malena's history class.

"Malena, this is our big chance to get back at them."

Kids brushed by them, some saying hello and others saying, "Get out of the way, stupids."

"You've changed your opinion," said Malena. "I thought you wanted me to back off."

"I know. Now I think we *should* get them back." She pushed at her glasses.

Malena leaned against the doorjamb. "I don't want revenge anymore. It makes me sick to my stomach."

"But it's not fair what they've done," said Yolanda.

What was fair?

Yolanda shifted her books. "Pray for me? I want to do good on that test." She hurried across the hall, and Malena went inside the classroom.

Jesse, the guy who sat across from her, perched on her desk. "Malena," he said, "will you pray for me?"

She glared at him. "What for?"

"Because I dream about you. I want you. I—"

She kicked him, and he jumped off the desk, laughing.

"Is this junior high or what?" asked the girl behind her.

"Worse. The insane asylum." Malena sat down as the tardy bell rang.

Ms. Reyes walked in, dressed like a pilgrim.

"I can't believe this." Malena put her head on her arms. The class groaned, and Ms. Reyes began her lesson about colonial times. Life was definitely an insane asylum.

At lunch, Malena and Yolanda met at Malena's locker. "I can't eat," said Yolanda. "I'm going to study in the library."

"You want me to quiz you?"

"No, it's okay."

So Malena walked to the junior-senior park alone. She felt funny being by herself. She couldn't find an unoccupied bench, so she sat on the grass and began to eat her sandwich. Peanut butter and honey, courtesy of Lucia.

Bruce appeared, holding his lunch tray. "Hey, *señorita.*"

"I thought you didn't know any Spanish."

"You just heard my vast vocabulary."

"I'm impressed."

"Thanks. Want company for lunch?"

"Sure."

He sat beside her on the dying grass. The harsh sunlight stung through the smog. In the distance Nadine's laughter carried to them. Malena didn't see her, so maybe it was another girl.

"Did you love her?" asked Malena suddenly.

Bruce looked up, surprised. "What?"

"Juliana. Did you love her?"

He looked thoughtful a moment. "Yeah, at least I thought I did. But maybe I really didn't after all."

"Do you feel weird about it? Like because you thought you loved someone and she turned out to be sort of a creep?" He looked surprised again, and she bit her lip. "You do think she's a creep, don't you? I hope I'm not saying anything too—"

He broke in. "No, you're right. I sometimes think that."

Malena put down her peanut butter sandwich. "I mean, like for me. My friends, you know, the ones who hate me now? I wonder if there is something really wrong with me for picking them. Maybe I have this self-destructive part of me. Why didn't I know they would be awful?"

"I don't think I was being self-destructive," said Bruce slowly. "I was just looking for some fun. I mean, I really liked Juliana, but then the whole thing sort of backfired."

They ate in silence. Malena busily thought of different scenarios, interchanging Nadine, Annie, Yolanda, and herself. What if she and Yolanda had acted first, pushing away the others' friendship because they didn't want to be with them anymore? Would she have been cruel to Nadine and Annie?

Why did they want her gone? That was the main question. She and Yolanda hadn't changed, had they? Nadine and Annie changed. But what made them change so drastically that they didn't want to be friends anymore?

When Malena finished her sandwich, she said, "I've been friends with Nadine since fourth grade. I met her just before Yolanda. I could see how they'd be awful if Yolanda and I had done something terrible to them, but we haven't." At least not that she knew of. Had they done something to Nadine and Annie and not known it?

Malena could still remember the first time she'd seen Nadine. They were two little skinny kids playing four square together, and they had beat everyone else. The two of them held their winning position for the whole school year. They had been heady, triumphant, such buddies.

"People do change," said Bruce. "That much I know."

Malena wondered if he was thinking of Juliana. "I guess I've changed," said Malena. "But I'm still me. I mean, I don't think the inside me has changed."

"Maybe you have and don't realize it," he said.

Was that it? So simple, yet so uncontrollable: change.

"Last year I got in a lot of trouble," said Malena. "I was into partying. Nadine got me into the party scene." It suddenly occurred to her that Nadine was still chasing after the parties, and she wasn't anymore. Was that part of the change Nadine hated?

"So what happened?" asked Bruce. "You're not partying now are you?"

She shook her head. "One night we got hauled in for being rowdy after curfew. Some of the kids had been smoking a little crack." She had been arrested too. That was before Rudy had quit crack, and he'd been with her.

Papa bailed her out. At four in the morning. The rain was slanting down and he came and got her. He hadn't yelled, but he just hunched over the steering wheel and looked so sad. She wanted to wash away with the rain.

Later, after she slept, Papa told her that she'd hurt him more than anyone ever had. She wanted to pat him on the back and say it was okay, but it wasn't okay. She wasn't okay.

Papa had said, "Lena, you have hurt me more than you can imagine. But you are hurting yourself even more."

"So what happened?" Bruce asked.

"I had to go to court and do all this volunteer work for the city. But I changed somewhere along the way. It wasn't that I was scared of getting caught. It was something deeper. Maybe because I'd hurt my papa."

And there was God in there, too, somehow keeping a hold on her, like she was a puppy on a long leash. He didn't really hold her tight. He just was there, hanging on, leading her gently. She knew a lot of it was because Peewee was praying for her. Maybe prayer was like the leash, holding her lightly.

Bruce tossed his cardboard tray in the trash can. "So there you are," he said. "You have changed, but your friends haven't. So they can't stand to be around you."

"But Yolanda hasn't changed. Why is she staying with me?"

He shrugged. "Maybe she's closer to the place you're at now."

That was probably true. Malena leaned against a tree. "Last year I used to see Juliana at parties sometimes."

"I know," said Bruce. "I had thought she wasn't partying anymore. She said she'd changed. But she changed back. Or probably she didn't really change."

"I think I'll stay where I've changed to," said Malena.

"How can you be sure?" he asked.

"I guess I can't. But I think about God more, and he's helped me change. I think he's on my side, you know?"

"No, actually, I don't know," said Bruce. "But I'd like to have God on my side, especially if God is really all-powerful. I can understand why parents want their kids to go to Sunday school. They want them to be okay, and they figure God will make their kids okay."

"I guess *you can* understand parents," she said. "How weird that seems."

Bruce laughed harshly. "I don't understand mine, though."

Malena sighed, put her elbows on her knees, and leaned her face into her palms. "I don't always understand mine, either."

The passing bell rang. They got up. Malena brushed grass and dirt off her skirt, and they walked back toward the C building.

Bruce touched her arm. "I promised you I'd tell someone. I'm gonna be talking to Juliana today after practice."

Malena nodded. "Where are you guys gonna talk?"

"I don't know yet."

"Can you go someplace I can get to?"

Bruce smiled a little. "You're really serious about not trusting her, aren't you?"

Malena nodded. Everything within her screamed that Juliana was up to something.

Bruce tipped his head, thinking, and Malena was embarrassed. She hoped he didn't think she was just jealous or some weird thing.

"How about the dam?" he said. "Where we went jogging. I'll get her to drive there to talk."

"I could use another jog," Malena said. "I won't bother you or anything. I'll just sort of jog by and see that you're okay."

"Okay." She watched him walk off, his blond hair standing out like a beacon among all the black-haired kids.

CHAPTER 22

Bruce

AFTER TRACK Bruce picked up his sweats and started back to the locker room to shower when Juliana appeared. "Come on," she called and waved at him from the infield.

"I need to shower," he called back.

She shook her head. "Let's go now," she said, smiling. "I don't have much time. Besides, I'm used to your sweat, you know." She gave him a bigger smile and he flushed.

So he let himself be led across the track to the student parking lot. He slipped into the passenger seat of the Camaro. The back seat was piled with junk, a familiar-looking sleeping bag, several blankets. "Moving out?" he teased, but he wondered what exactly she had in mind.

She laughed, sounding like she used to. "Gotta take that stuff inside. I keep forgetting. Let's go back to my house, okay?"

He shook his head, though the idea was tempting. Quickly, he squelched it. *Don't be a fool, Evans,* he told himself. *Do you really think you two can get back together?* He could hope, couldn't he?

He groaned softly. He was a hopeless case. Then remembering what he'd told Malena, he said, "Let's go over to the dam. I've been running some of the trails."

For a moment she looked strangely pleased. But all she said was, "The dam it is."

As she drove, she chatted about school, her parents, the new horse she was riding, "A big black hellion. I have to get after him all the time."

They pulled into the small gravel parking lot on top of the earthen dam above the Rio Hondo riverbed. "Let's walk," she said. They walked down the steep hill to the riverbed where he and Malena had jogged.

A car door slammed above from the parking lot. Bruce looked up. So did Juliana, but then she looked away, pointing at the river. "Look how low the water is."

He started to ask if she had heard the car door, but she chattered on. He started to tell her a little about Zachary.

She shook her head. "I don't want to talk about the baby."

"What do you want to talk about then?"

She gave him a suggestive look and stopped in the middle of the trail. Heavy bushes surrounded them, obscuring the dam, the road, everything but the trail in front and behind them. "Don't you know?" She reached over and began kissing him.

He stepped back startled, surprised, but glad because he hoped it would be this way. He'd missed her. No, he missed her body. He'd missed how soft her lips were. He put his arms around her waist.

Suddenly, he was grabbed from behind.

Juliana sprang out of his arms. "Hold him tight," she commanded.

Bruce struggled, but the person behind him twisted his arms tight, then tripped him. Bruce fell face first in the deep sand. Sand went up his nose and in his mouth. He raised his head, spitting.

Someone tied his wrists together, then he was flipped onto his back. *Derek,* Juliana's new boyfriend. Derek quickly tied Bruce's feet together with rope. Bruce couldn't believe how stupid he'd been. Betrayed with a kiss, the old plot.

"Hello," said Derek, showing his teeth. His long hair swung in Bruce's face. Bruce spat sand at him, but Derek was too far away.

"No wonder you had so much junk in your backseat," said Bruce sourly. All the time Derek had been buried there. He had probably been there the other times Juliana had tried to pick him up. How could Bruce have been so stupid? Because he wanted to believe Juliana and he could get back together.

Juliana tipped her head. "Derek and I have a present for you, Bruce."

Derek pulled a cigarette and a disposable lighter out of his shirt pocket. Handing the cigarette to Juliana, he lit it for her.

Bruce struggled, but Derek pressed his boot on Bruce's chest. "Hold still."

"You gonna kill me or what?" asked Bruce through clenched teeth.

Juliana blew out a stream of smoke. "The 'or what.'" She pushed up his shirt sleeve. Slowly, she pulled the cigarette out of her mouth and held the lit end close to his arm. The heat prickled his skin. He struggled again, but Derek held him down.

"Just a little brand," Juliana said. "To warn other girls about you. Brands don't hurt horses much, so don't worry."

He started to protest that she was to blame as much as him, but she pressed the end of the cigarette against his upper arm.

Pain. Scarlet, blistering pain. Cigarettes burned at 450 degrees Fahrenheit, he had read somewhere. The burning from that tiny spot cleared his mind of every other thought. The smell of his burned flesh seared his nostrils.

Juliana backed off, laughing. She looked at Derek. "That wasn't so difficult," she said.

Derek started to let Bruce go.

"Wait," she said. "I'm not done."

"Okay," said Bruce. The pain stabbed him fiercely. "You've had your fun. Let me go now."

"I told you I was going to brand you to warn other girls, and I mean it. Hold him, Derek."

"Come on, Juliana. You got him," said Derek.

Juliana gave him a furious look. "I haven't gotten him enough."

Bruce refused to appeal to her. Once before he'd seen her very angry when her father was supposed to pick her up for her birthday and take her out to dinner. He never showed up. Bruce went over to console her, and when he got to her house, she had torn up all her photos of her father and broken the glass animal collection her father had given her when she was a kid. He'd hurt her, failed her. Now she had the same kind of frenzied look on her face.

"Hold him," snapped Juliana. She threw back her long hair and took a drag on the cigarette as Derek stepped on Bruce's arm and planted his other foot on Bruce's chest.

Bruce hit at Derek's leg with his head, but Derek only kicked back. It made Bruce's head ring. He closed his eyes, preparing for the pain.

Someone yelled.

Suddenly the pressure lifted off his arm and chest.

He opened his eyes. Juliana jumped over him, and Derek was stumbling away. Juliana dropped the cigarette in the sand beside him. Bruce jerked away from it.

Two guys ran by Bruce, thundering after Juliana and Derek. Bruce recognized the lanky body of his teammate, Matt, and that earring-studded friend of Malena's, Rudy.

Then Malena knelt beside him. "You idiot," she said, untying his hands and legs.

"What took you so long?" he asked. Then to his embarrassment he passed out, not from pain, but from acute relief.

CHAPTER 23

Malena

MALENA WOKE to the sound of fine rain. She sat up and yawned. Lucia wasn't in the bedroom, but the mutter of the television floating under her door told her where her sister lurked. For a moment Malena thought it was just another Saturday.

After they'd rescued Bruce, Matt drove Bruce home. He was the one who had driven Malena and Rudy to the dam. Rudy and Matt had chased Juliana and Derek through the bamboo stands and told them that Bruce was calling the police and pressing charges. Juliana actually was crying. Probably more from being caught—again—than from any guilt. Sadness had sifted into Malena's thoughts. She actually felt sorry for Juliana.

Then, as she had walked home alone into the dusk, the swift feeling of having to do something about Nadine and Annie encircled her. *You think you're a fancy hero? Ha! Not until you forgive Nadine and Annie and try and make things better.*

Why did she have such a persistent conscience?

Malena stumbled into the shower, and when she was dressed again, she went into the kitchen. Papa worked on Saturdays, but Mama didn't. She was folding laundry now in the living room. Lucia, Ramon, and Carlos were helping her, though mostly they were staring at television cartoons.

Malena plopped down at the kitchen table and dialed Bruce's house before she lost her nerve. His uncle answered and called for Bruce. In the background music played. What was it? She thought it was an old Moody Blues song.

"Hello?" Bruce's voice sounded distant.

"It's me, Malena. How are you?" The baby let loose a squeal in the background.

"Fine, thanks to you and Matt and Rudy."

"Your arm okay?"

"Yeah, it's not that bad of a burn. I'll live." A pause. "I haven't told my uncle about any of it. If I do, he'll want me to press charges."

Malena swung the telephone cord. Ramon, Lucia, and Mom were laughing together in the other room. "You don't want to?" She thought he probably should, especially since they'd told Juliana and Derek they would.

"I'm not sure. I don't know." He paused, his breathing rattled over the phone. Then the baby squealed again.

She took a deep breath. "Can I ask a favor of you?" said Malena.

"Anything."

"Hmm, I better take advantage of this, no?" she said. Bruce chuckled, and she went on. "Would you come over here to my house while I find the stuff that's Nadine's, then go with me over to her place?"

"Why? You gonna kill her?" He sounded amused.

"No." Malena was surprised to realize how calm she felt, like a level stretch of water running smooth, not churning. At least not at this moment.

"I'll have to bring Zachary," he said.

"That's okay."

"See you in an hour. How's that?"

"No problem." They hung up, and Malena wandered out into the living room and helped fold and hang up clothes. She wasn't sure why she wanted Bruce rather than Yolanda with her. She just knew that she did.

"Enough TV," said Mama finally. She flicked it off, and Carlos squealed in protest.

"Aw, Mama," said Ramon.

"I really, really want to watch that," said Lucia.

"Too bad. Go outside and play," said Mama.

They went out grumbling but didn't seem that upset.

"Is it okay if Bruce and his baby come over?" she asked. The night before, she had told her parents about Juliana and Derek and what they had done.

Papa had snorted. "As if there aren't enough problems in the world—no, these two have to stir more problems up."

Mama had put her hand on Malena's shoulder and said, "We're proud of you, helping this boy."

Malena was embarrassed by their reaction but pleased at the same time. She'd only done what any friends would do. Yet would she have helped Nadine or Annie? She wasn't so sure.

Mama nodded and folded a shirt of Papa's. "It's good to be friends with Bruce. He probably needs friends now."

The fresh, clean scent of warm clothes circled the living room. "Mama," Malena said, "is there anyone you ever really hated? Someone you wanted to hurt?"

Mama shook out a sheet and neatly folded it. She was quiet for a long moment. Malena could see Mama going back in time in her thoughts. "Yes, there was someone. His name was Donnie McNeil. Funny I can remember his name."

Malena stretched out on her side on the scratchy carpet, propping her head up with her hand. "Why did you hate him?"

"He was cruel to me. When we crossed the border, we first lived in Calexico. I was only Carlos's age. This boy was in my first grade class. I didn't know much English, and for that he teased me."

"Why didn't the teacher make him stop?" Malena asked, fascinated. Mama was always so outspoken and fiery. Malena was amazed to think of her as a timid child.

"This Donnie only teased me when the teacher wasn't looking. He would tell me I was a dumb taco. That much English I understood. Then he started pushing me, and I'd fall down on the hard ground. My knees and hands would bleed. And none of the other children would help me because they were afraid of him, too."

Malena had told Bruce that God was on their side, but where was God for Mama? "Did you want to kill Donnie?" asked Malena.

"Oh, yes. But he was too strong. Then when I joined second grade he found another child to be cruel to. I'm ashamed that I did nothing to stop him. I was only grateful it wasn't me he picked on."

"Oh, Mama. You were a little kid. What could you have done?"

Mama shrugged and picked up the pile of bath towels. "I could have told a teacher. But I didn't. I feel sorry for him now. He must have been an unhappy boy." Mama walked into the bathroom and put away the towels.

Was Nadine unhappy? Was Annie unhappy? Malena wrinkled her nose, thinking. What would Nadine be unhappy about? Well, her brother was the leader of the

Metal Jungle. That was bad enough. Also her papa had vanished years ago. Annie lived with both her parents, but her parents yelled at each other a lot. But then everyone had things to be unhappy about. Maybe it boiled down to not having someone who believed in you or not believing in Someone who was greater than all your bad fortune.

There was a knock at the front door. As Malena jumped up, Ramon's voice floated in from the open window next to the door. "Are you my sister's boyfriend?"

She'd kill him.

Then Lucia's high voice. "Why are you carrying that baby?"

Bruce answered softly and Malena couldn't catch the words.

Malena opened the front door. Lucia stood with a jump rope in her hands, and Ramon sat on his bike, grinning broadly. "Go play, Ramon," Malena ordered. He darted off with his pack of little friends but not before chanting, "Malena's boyfriend! Malena has a boyfriend!"

"Ignore him," said Malena. "He is a complete pest."

Zachary was looking around curiously as Bruce walked through the front door. "I never had any brothers or sisters," Bruce said.

"You are incredibly lucky." Malena wished passionately that she was an only child.

"Maybe," said Bruce. Zachary squealed, still looking around.

Malena introduced Mama to Bruce.

"Look at the baby," said Mama, holding her hands out. Bruce handed the baby over, grinning like a fool.

For a brief, scared moment Malena wondered how Bruce would see their shabby house, the stained carpet, the old furniture. But Bruce talked with Mama and told her about Zachary. He wasn't looking around, gawking, or staring, so Malena relaxed. It was okay.

When Mama gave the baby back to Bruce, she offered to warm a bottle because Zachary was starting to fuss a little. Then Malena and Bruce went into her room. He laid the baby on the floor, a blanket under him, and said, "What kind of help do you need?"

She sat on the edge of her bed, biting one of her fingernails. "Mostly moral support, I think. I have a bunch of Nadine's stuff, and I need to return it. At first I thought I'd just keep it all, but now I think I should return it."

He nodded. "You can sort of be calling a truce." Sunlight from the window found his blonde hair. It was exactly the color of Zachary's fuzz, almost white, like the corona around the sun. Malena wondered if he had a way to call a truce with Juliana—though it seemed as if he had, but she wasn't accepting it.

For the next half hour Malena went through her closet, dresser drawers, and under her bed until she had two shopping bags full of sweaters, blouses, makeup, and music tapes. She held up a red sweater. "This was my total favorite. I thought about, you know, just keeping it, but then if I wore it, I'd know and she'd know."

Bruce nodded seriously. Mama had brought the warmed bottle, and Bruce sat on the floor, feeding the baby. When Zachary finished the bottle, they left the house, Bruce carrying the baby and Malena carrying her bags.

"Her apartment is just a couple blocks away," Malena said as they went out the front door. Ramon and his friends zoomed by on bikes, standing on the pedals, screeching like banshees. Lucia was playing hopscotch with Yolanda's little sisters. Carlos stood before the girls, demanding, "I want to play!"

"No boys," the girls kept saying. Then Carlos would beg Ramon to let him ride on the handle bars.

"You're too little," Ramon would say.

Carlos stamped his feet, furious.

Malena was about to take Carlos with them when Lucia came up and said kindly, "You can take my turn, Carlos."

Malena and Bruce watched the little boy toss the marker and hop through the squares. Then they turned to go.

"Don't step on any cracks," Lucia warned them. "Or bad things will happen."

"Bad things have already happened," Malena said.

Lucia's expression hardened. "I know. But it helps to try." Malena thought Lucia must be getting past her legalistic phase.

"Other ways are better." Malena pointed up.

Carlos hopped over and said, "She means God, don't you, Malena?"

"Yeah."

"That's right," said Bruce. "If God's on your side, who can be against you?"

He and Malena laughed high-spiritedly. Malena was pleased Bruce had remembered their conversation. Lucia stared after them, her mouth open. Malena knew she'd hear about this tonight, but that was okay. Anyway, it was time for Lucia to stop being superstitious. And, she thought, time for me to quit ignoring God so much.

Suddenly Bruce stopped laughing, as they saw Juliana and Derek walking down the street, away from Nadine's apartment.

CHAPTER 24

Bruce

BRUCE'S WHOLE BODY went rigid, and the burn on his upper arm suddenly blossomed with pain. What were they doing here? What if they got hold of Zachary? That was a totally scary thought.

"Come on," said Malena. "They haven't seen us yet. Let's sit here a moment." She led him to some steps leading onto a porch. When they sat, the evergreen hedges hid them and blocked their view.

Bruce lay the baby on his lap, and Zachary waved his arms and feet.

"What I want to know is why they're here," said Malena. "Drugs, maybe. But it's too coincidental, them by Nadine's."

Despite the splash of sunlight, Bruce felt chilled. What if they were after Malena now? This had to stop. "Look, I better go and leave you alone," he said.

"Why?"

"I don't want to get you in any more trouble." This was his battle. She'd saved him once. That was enough.

She remained calm and put her hand on his arm. "Sit down, Bruce." He hadn't gotten up. Yet. "We're in this together somehow. We'll think of something."

He must be a wimp, letting a girl bail him out. But he really didn't want to leave. He looked over the top of the evergreen bushes. He didn't see Juliana or Derek. Malena stood and he followed. The streets were free of white people. Only a couple of Hispanic kids shot by on bikes.

"Let's go," said Malena.

Bruce shouldered Zachary, who was falling asleep despite all the excitement. They walked another block until Malena halted in front of a triplex.

"She lives here," said Malena. "In the first apartment. This is weird. I haven't been here in weeks. I used to be here almost every day."

A black pitbull with a bolt of white on her chest barked at them from the front yard. Zachary jerked his arms.

"Hey, Babe," called Malena. The dog stopped barking and wagged her whip tail.

Malena opened the gate and Bruce followed her in, wondering if he was a good parent walking into a yard with a strange pitbull. Babe wriggled over to them, and Malena stroked the dog's ears. "It's okay," she said. "Babe's friendly. As long as she knows you."

Oh, great. Bruce tightened his grip on the baby, who followed the dog with his gaze. Babe sniffed Bruce's legs carefully and looked up at him with big dark eyes. "Good dog," Bruce said, walking quickly behind Malena.

The dog let him go. Malena stopped at the door of the first apartment and knocked. Flowered curtains, looking suspiciously like bedsheets, hung from the front windows. Malena actually looked frightened.

Bruce bumped her with his arm. He didn't say it, but he hoped she understood: If you fall, I'll catch you.

Babe nuzzled the plastic shopping bags Malena held, making them crackle. The dog barked again, and the front door opened with Nadine behind the screen. Nadine's eyes widened. Babe barked harder and jumped on the screen door.

"Down," ordered Nadine. The dog ignored her and barked harder. Nadine yelled for someone. "Come get your dog!"

A boy ran out past her between Malena and Bruce. He grabbed the dog, and they wrestled on the grass together.

"So what do you want?" asked Nadine. She didn't look quite as pretty as usual.

Bruce shifted the baby and Nadine glared at him.

"These are yours," said Malena holding out the bags. "Stuff I've borrowed. I didn't want you to think I was gonna keep them."

Nadine opened the door again to take the bags and Bruce caught a whiff of perfume, so familiar. His heart stopped. It was Juliana's perfume. He'd know it anywhere. So Juliana and Derek had been talking to Nadine.

He shifted Zachary to his arm, fighting the impulse to blab what he was thinking. His mind ran in various directions, trying to explain it. Of course Nadine just happened to wear Juliana's perfume. Why not? Except it was totally expensive, and a girl who lived in a house with sheets for curtains probably couldn't buy it. Maybe Nadine stole it. Or had a rich boyfriend. Maybe. So why was Juliana walking down Nadine's street?

Nadine stared at him as if she were reading his thoughts like a computer spreadsheet. "That kid really don't look like Juliana," Nadine said finally.

Bruce lifted his head proudly. "He's half mine."

Nadine raised her eyebrows but didn't say anything more. She looked into the two bags.

"It's all there," Malena murmured.

Nadine smirked. "Just making sure it's not dog crap or something."

Malena's eyes snapped.

Zachary drooled on Bruce's arm. Babe was barking again, happy with her boy as they ran up and down the lawn.

Nadine tossed the bags inside and turned to go in. Bruce backed up.

But Malena persisted, her face earnest. "We probably can't be friends again," she said, "but I'll never be sorry that we *were* friends."

Nadine paused a moment, blinked, then softly pushed the door shut.

Malena turned and jerked her chin away from the door. "Let's go."

Bruce was glad to leave.

Malena called good-bye to the boy and Babe. Then Bruce walked out with Malena, the iron-work gate slamming behind them. Babe barked madly after them, running along the fence line. They were out of the yard and now enemies.

Malena practically ran down the street. Bruce jogged after her with Zachary holding his head up to the breeze, grinning his gummy grin to the wind.

"Let's go see a friend of mine," Malena said, slowing for him. "He might be able to give us some answers."

Bruce felt a flutter of jealousy but squelched it. He and Malena were friends, and friends let friends have their own lives and other friends. He swallowed and said, "Sure." Then he followed her down the street. He found himself nervously looking for blond heads.

The wind carried the scent of the riverbed, murky water, damp soil, decaying plants. He wrinkled his nose.

Zachary squirmed and finally Bruce stopped so he could put the baby in the backpack.

Malena walked about half a block before she realized they weren't with her. She hurried back. "Sorry."

"Stressful time, huh?" he asked.

Malena stood on one foot, then the other. "I guess I hoped Nadine and I could be friends again. That's dumb, no?"

He thought of himself kissing Juliana. "Not dumb, just hopeful."

Malena bit her lower lip. "I wonder why she was seeing Juliana and Derek."

"Drugs?" he asked.

Malena shook her head, her long hair sweeping over her back. "Nadine's not connected. No, I'm worried about the Metal Jungle. Nadine's brother is the leader, you know."

"What's that got to do with—," Bruce swallowed, suddenly getting it. "You mean like a contract? They are taking a contract out on us?"

"Money can get you almost anything," said Malena.

Bruce stared in shock at various people on the street. Like in a Woody Allen movie, he felt like asking them, "Did you know a gang might be after me? What should I do?" They would probably advise him to buy a gun. Great, a life of crime was beckoning to him. All because of one small baby. Was that weird or what? Zachary kicked him a few times until Bruce grabbed his feet. Zachary giggled.

"He's sure happy," said Malena.

"Good thing," said Bruce. "He cries and screams enough as it is. I can't imagine if he did it all the time."

After a moment Malena said, "My friend who might be able to help us lives in the riverbed."

Bruce frowned. "What do you mean?"

"He lives most of the time under the bridge, the overpass, you know?"

"But why?" Bruce had visions of a bagperson pushing around a shopping cart filled with cans, newspapers, and other filthy junk. Why was Malena friends with someone like that?

"Because he helps people. He says the best way he can do that is to live like them."

Bruce knew he was flinching.

Malena laughed lightly. "I know. It sounds horrible, doesn't it? But you'll like Peewee, I think. And he knows what's going down."

Bruce wasn't crazy about bringing the baby with him. What if this Peewee had AIDS or something? He didn't want the baby catching something gross.

"Remember how we talked about changing and God being on our side? Well, God is on Peewee's side and he changed Peewee, so Peewee loves the street people," Malena explained.

Who'd want to live with drunks and loadies? Not him.

"It's okay, Bruce." Malena brushed his arm with her hand. "God doesn't force anyone."

He still cringed at the thought of Peewee's life. Then he thought, *What a jerk you are, Evans. Sure, you got money and these people don't.*

He didn't even want to entertain those thoughts. What if he got too compassionate? He might do something like join them. No, never. He had enough trouble taking care of one little baby—but wasn't *that* peculiar? How many sixteen-year-old boys kept their babies? None that he knew. So was this his change? But how? Or rather why? He'd never asked to be changed. Or had he?

"Let's stop here a second," said Malena. She walked into a Carl's Jr. and ordered food. "Can I bum off you, Bruce?"

He gave her more than she needed, but she handed back his change. He took it because he didn't want to humiliate her. They walked back onto the streets, Malena cradling the bag of food.

"For your friend?" he asked.

"Yeah."

Bruce wanted to ask, Doesn't God feed him? But as he thought about it, he realized that this guy *was* being fed—by Malena.

The street before the riverbed held rundown houses with peeling paint and sagging porches. Half-dead trees poked up from the dirt lawns. Paper trash curled against fences and huddled beside curbs. A few low-rider cars sat on the street, but mostly rusted-out, cheap Japanese cars sat on the dirt lawns and against the curb.

Bruce studied Malena walking unconcerned along the street. Was it that she didn't care? No, she just accepted it. Was it acceptance or just part of her life, something she didn't think twice about? In any event, she just walked on and Bruce continued to follow. At the edge of the overpass crossing the river, a chain-link fence bound the city out except for a small entryway. Malena slipped through, and he followed.

Smog hung like a dirty curtain in the distance. Bruce couldn't even see through the haze beyond the next bridge. But birds sang gaily and swooped along the bushes that grew up the sides of the broken cement which shaped the flood control. A couple kids on bikes whizzed by over the packed dirt.

"Under here," said Malena. She walked down the cemented path under the bridge. Broken glass shone up and down the path, sparkling like stars in a clear night sky.

"Peewee," she called. "Are you here?"

Mattresses, pillows, a barbecue grill and other junk sat under the bridge next to the thick supports.

Bruce wrinkled his nose at the stench. "Isn't it illegal to live here?" asked Bruce. Then he felt stupid. Of course it was. But what were the other choices?

Malena didn't embarrass him by answering. "I wonder where he—" She gasped and grabbed Bruce's arm. "Look!" She pointed out onto the water. "It's a heron."

A big gray-blue bird rose out of the water. Huge, with flapping wings tipped in dark gray, it had to have been half as tall as Bruce, its long legs trailing behind it. The heron croaked hoarsely as it flew.

"I'm amazed that birds this beautiful live here," she said, picking her way back down to the cement path. "I could leave Peewee's food there and hope a dog doesn't get it. Or the crows."

Bruce imagined a cluster of crows eating a Carl's Jr. hamburger.

"Look," said Malena. She pointed north down the trail. Bruce looked for another bird but only saw a guy walking toward them.

Malena bounded up the cement path to the other side of the trail. Bruce followed. Zachary was quiet, so Bruce looked over his shoulder. The baby was sleeping, his head lolling to one side. Malena skipped down the trail like a little kid, her hair flopping. Bruce felt like an old man, following her around.

Malena met up with the guy and talked, her voice not carrying to Bruce, but she was gesturing and pointing, first at the river—the heron—and then at Bruce. Soon Bruce caught up to them.

Peewee was thin, not much taller than Malena, and he had bright, kind eyes. "So this is Bruce," he said. "And the little one, no?"

Bruce turned to show him the baby sleeping in his pack.

Malena gave Peewee the food. "From Bruce and me."

"Thank you." Peewee sat down in the sunshine, leaning against a brick wall that separated the apartment complex from the riverbed.

Bruce decided to leave the pack on. Better if the baby slept. He certainly didn't want Zachary crawling around on the dirt and glass. He sat carefully in the shade of a tree near Peewee. Malena plopped down in the dust next to Peewee.

"I'm glad to see you," said Peewee around mouthfuls of burger. He waved to a couple of kids on skateboards who waved back and rattled under the bridge.

"So what do you think of this world?" asked Peewee.

"It's awful," said Bruce.

Peewee put down the drink and said seriously, "You are exactly right. And you know what else is awful?"

The light in Peewee's eyes made Bruce not want to know.

"I've been hearing things about you two."

"What things?" Malena asked quickly. She glanced at Bruce.

"I heard two white people want to get some revenge on a Mexican girl and a white boy." Peewee licked the salt from his fingers.

"Us," said Bruce.

"Juliana and Derek," said Malena. Her eyes grew hard.

"That's right," said Peewee. "What's going on?"

Bruce told Peewee what had happened the day before. He had a feeling that little of it was new to Peewee. Bruce also told him about the baby, about Juliana, about his parents, about his father kicking him out and about his uncle helping him.

Peewee listened quietly, eating, nodding his head.

Way to go, Evans, he thought when he was finished. He hoped he'd never be interrogated. He'd tell all.

"So Juliana and Derek are asking the Metal Jungle for help?" asked Malena.

Bruce's stomach tightened at the mention of the gang's name.

"They've been asking for Angel, but you know Angel. He don't talk to just anyone." Peewee carefully folded the Carl's Jr. bag.

"So are they gonna get to talk to Angel?" asked Malena.

Peewee shrugged. "It's up to Nadine, I think. Angel, he knows what's coming down, but he won't do anything unless Nadine gives him the word."

"Because Nadine and I are enemies?" asked Malena.

Peewee shrugged. "That's what I hear."

"Who told you all this?" asked Bruce. "How did he know?"

Peewee licked his fingers again. "A couple of guys in Metal Jungle are friends of mine. I helped them and now they help me."

Malena explained what they'd seen on their way to Nadine's.

"That's right," said Peewee. "Pretty little Nadine holds the key, I'd say."

Bruce bit the inside of his mouth. Maybe he could go far away, like back to Colorado Springs to visit Mom's parents. Malena could come along, too. His grandparents were always inviting him to visit. Well, he'd visit for two years, then go to college anywhere but California. He grew angry, furious, that Juliana could cause so much trouble.

"Did Nadine agree to talk to her brother?" asked Malena.

"You ask me?" said Peewee. "You just came from her."

"I don't know," said Malena.

"Especially now it's possible, no?" asked Peewee.

"Especially now," said Malena.

Peewee turned to Bruce. "Do you think you can change the white girl's mind?"

Bruce played with a handful of pebbles. "I'm not sure. I could try. But she's awfully mad. I might make it worse." He figured Juliana would just laugh at him and see his plea as a sign of weakness.

Would cops be able to do anything? he wondered. Probably not, except he could at least press charges. But if Juliana had already set in motion a plan for the Metal Jungle to come after them, it would be too late. What could the police do? Set up a 24-hour guard? Hardly.

Malena was twisting a lock of hair. "If I could just get Nadine to not talk to her brother. . . . The Metal Jungle only do what they want. They don't care about anyone else's revenge, unless it's for one of their own. Like Nadine's pride or something."

"Not even for money?" asked Bruce.

Malena and Peewee seemed to consider the idea. Malena finally said, "It's possible, but because Nadine is involved, it's probably up to her."

Peewee nodded. "Talk to Nadine then."

"She hates me," said Malena. She put her head in her arms.

Peewee shrugged. "But once Nadine loved you, no?"

Malena just looked out over the river.

Zachary stirred and made funny squeaking noises.

"They might hurt my baby," said Bruce. Maybe he really should get out of the city for a while.

Peewee stared at him as if to say that they might.

Bruce wondered what happened to God being for them? Wouldn't that mean that he'd protect them, especially a little baby? But then what about kids who get killed in wars and stuff. They didn't get protected.

"I'll try and talk to Nadine," said Malena.

"When?" asked Bruce. "Tonight?"

Malena shook her head. "No. She likes to go out and party. I better not bug her then. She'd be furious and probably not help just because of that. Her mom usually makes her go to mass. I'll talk to her then."

Peewee nodded, his skinny neck bobbing like a turkey's. "You aren't alone, you know," he said.

Malena, still twisting her hair, closed her eyes a minute. Was she praying right then, Bruce wondered.

"People do change," Malena said slowly. "We'll ask for that in our prayers."

Bruce wished certain people would change the state they lived in. That would certainly help things.

Malena kissed Peewee's cheek and said something to him in Spanish. Then Bruce and she walked off the riverbed. She waved to Peewee, who waved back. The baby yelped a couple of times, then settled down. Bruce hated to admit it, but he was intensely glad to be leaving.

After they crossed the bridge, Bruce asked, "What did you say to Peewee?"

"You really don't know any Spanish?"

"Sorry, just German." Bruce felt like a dumb tourist.

"I just told him that I loved him," she said.

Bruce marveled at the craziness of that. This was all so crazy. He wondered what tomorrow would be like. Would the Metal Jungle be closing in on him?

Please God, keep the baby, Malena, and me safe, okay?

Then he wondered why God should care? But he hoped that in some crazy, inexplicable way God did care.

CHAPTER 25

Bruce Again

AN EXPLOSION startled Bruce awake. Gun shot.

He sat up, shaking in the pale dawn, trying to determine whether he was dreaming or not. Then as a car rumbled outside and he ran the sound through his brain again, he realized that it had been a car backfiring. He slept again and dreamed of the Death Angel, who had a face like Juliana.

When he woke, Zachary was giving impatient cries.

As Bruce changed the baby, he thought about all the things he wanted to do: go to college, maybe be a teacher, get married, have a real family. But most of all he wished his own family would get back together.

"We need to visit your grandparents," he told Zachary. That's what he could do, try to visit them. His parents slept in late on Sunday mornings, then went out for brunch. They would be home by two.

After feeding the baby, he tried to study. Zachary scooted around on the floor, drooling onto the carpet.

But Bruce couldn't concentrate. He kept wondering how it was going with Malena and Nadine. *Just this once, God,* he thought. *Make it work out, okay? I'll never ask you for anything again.*

But he knew that wouldn't be true. If God helped once, he'd be stupid not to ask again. Besides, if God was so great, keeping Bruce's head intact despite attacks from a former friend and lover shouldn't be too big an order.

He stared at his advanced algebra and wished he had three wishes: One—to take care of the Metal Jungle and Juliana situation; two—to get his parents and him get back together; and three—to get Malena's ex-friends to leave her alone.

He dumped his homework on his desk while the baby studied his toes. Then he picked up the phone to see if he could drop by his parents' house.

CHAPTER 26

Malena

MALENA AND HER FAMILY filed into St. Benedict's Church. Late as always. She clenched her teeth, furious. She'd have to sit through mass before she talked to Nadine.

The congregation numbered over two hundred people. The heady scent of incense swirled down the aisle. After her parents, she dipped her fingers into the cold holy water, crossed herself, and walked carefully down the middle aisle because the ends were full. Her family filed in. Papa and Mama before her, the rest of the kids behind.

Malena paused at the aisle Mama and Papa slid into, her bent knee touching the rough carpet. Then she sat down on the hard, wooden pew.

The familiar service, sitting, kneeling, standing, singing, praying, soothed her. Part of her respected the silent, strong-seeming priests of God who wore such beautiful colors except at Lent when all was repressed. But part of her hated mass with its boring liturgy.

Malena searched for Nadine and her family in the ocean of people. The organ music vibrated, and people rose to sing. Malena craned her neck, looking. *Be here, Nadine.*

Mama elbowed her and mouthed, "Pay attention."

Malena tried.

After another bout of kneeling and standing, Malena leaned back in the pew, pretending to stretch, but she looked quickly around.

Under the stained-glass window of Saint Francis of Assisi, red, purple, and blue light spilling over the rows, was a familiar head. Nadine was drenched in red light, the color of sin.

The service progressed, and Malena went up to the front of the church with her parents and Ramon for communion. Carlos and Lucia waited in the pews. Malena knew she shouldn't take communion today. Talk about sin in her heart. But it was more awkward not to because Mama and Papa would grill her: What did you do, *mi hija?*

Malena waited for communion at the foot of the altar with others, twisting to see Nadine from the front. Mama gave her a furious glare. Malena held still, but out of the corner of her eye she saw Nadine again, drenched in the red light, and Malena was deeply ashamed. Of course. Red was the color of blood, too, the color of forgiveness. Her heart ached sharply for a moment.

Father Carbajol made his way around the gathering of people at the foot of the altar, offering wafers. Malena liked him. He had taught her catechism class. She opened her mouth. The wafer touched her tongue, never her teeth, with its dry, gummy taste. Then the priest came with the blood-red wine. She sipped it. The warm, strong wine burned her throat.

Now, maybe her heart would be freed.

Malena followed her parents back down the aisle, quickly glancing around for Nadine. Nadine's mother went forward for communion, but Nadine rose and walked back down the aisle. Malena couldn't just watch her leave.

"I have to go to the bathroom," she whispered to Mama, keeping her eye on Nadine. She didn't go outside the church but through the back door to the courtyard.

Mama glared. "Hold it."

Malena opened her eyes wide. "It's not that."

Mama rolled her eyes. "Hurry up then."

Malena grabbed her little black purse and slipped out, hurrying down the aisle and out the back door.

The courtyard was smooth with high cement walls. During the school week when the nuns cared for them, the children played out here. Bright wild flowers grew along the wall and in the cracks of the cement.

The song of young children rang out from the nursery's open window. Malena slid away from the singing, down a hallway. She passed the silent kitchen. Coffee and plastic cups sat on long tables.

Malena slipped in, looking for Nadine. She didn't see anyone.

Not finding Nadine, she slipped back out in the dim hall, past the stairs that lead up to the crow's nest where Father Gomez held midweek studies for elementary-age kids. She used to go with Nadine and Yolanda. Once a long, long time ago. She pushed open the door to the girls' bathroom. Pipes gurgled. One of the stall doors was shut.

A toilet flushed, and a moment later Nadine walked out of the stall.

CHAPTER 27

Bruce

LIFE WOULD BE A LOT EASIER with a car, Bruce thought.
Even without track practice he was getting more than
enough exercise. Besides, walking took time that he
didn't always have. His grades had dropped since Zachary's birth but not as bad as he thought they might.
And not as bad as his parents gloomily predicted.

His parents.

His father was so exacting. Dinner at five-thirty. Mom
always had dinner ready then. She was the mistress of
the dinner game, always on time. Even when she'd had
some minor surgery, the next day she had dinner on the
table at five-thirty. Mom would say, "That's one reason
I can't work outside the home. I have to get dinner on
the table at five-thirty."

That was a scary thought.

He was glad to be away from his parents because with
them he was trapped. They were trapped, too, but they

didn't seem to notice or care. Yet they said that he would be trapped by the baby.

Well, wasn't it his choice to decide what would trap him? The baby wasn't a trap, anyway, not like a cage for a wild animal. Rather, Bruce keeping Zachary was more like a horse willingly allowing someone to harness him so he could help in the work.

Bruce walked fast through the hilly streets. Smog drifted in, obscuring everything a block or more away. Maybe that was why people went crazy in the city. There was no perspective.

On his block he slowed. Every crack in the sidewalk was familiar, the outline of every house, trees blooming on the front lawns. Everything was familiar, like coming home after a long journey.

Zachary dozed peacefully in the pack. Bruce wondered if the baby would remember any of this when he was older. "Sure, Dad, I remember you walking all over the place and me in the backpack, and I thought great thoughts and pooped a lot."

Well, Zachary sure did the last thing.

Bruce strode up his parents' driveway. Dad's shiny, red BMW sat in the drive. A pimply faced college student hand waxed it every week.

For a moment Bruce almost turned around and went back. *Don't be a wimp, Evans.* Taking a deep breath like he did before running a race, he knocked on the front door.

A slight shuffle whispered beyond the door. He knew Mom was looking through the peephole to be sure no ax murderer—she claimed she could tell by looking at the person—stood on her door step. He waved at the peephole.

The door opened. "Bruce!" As if she didn't know he was coming over. A little acting job to convince Dad this wasn't set up?

"Hi, Mom."

She touched his arm. "I've missed you, son."

Tears sprang to his eyes. "I've missed you, too."

She stepped back, eyeing the baby in the pack as Bruce crossed the door frame. "Your father is reading the paper," she told him. They paused in the entryway.

Of course. After their brunch, he read the hefty *Los Angeles Times.*

Mom moved ahead and he followed in her wake. "Bruce is here," she called.

Dad would probably think he came by for money.

Bruce stopped in the living room doorway by the big-screen television.

Dad looked up from the newspaper. "What's the matter? Justin kick you out?" Dad asked.

Be calm, Bruce told himself. "No," he said. "Uncle Justin has told me I can stay as long as I like. I just wanted to get a couple of books." He didn't say "my books" in case Dad would launch into a "nothing-is-yours-I-paid-for-it-all" bit.

What a true chicken, Evans! Tell him you wanted to see them, see him.

Dad just grunted and went back to the newspaper.

And Bruce didn't say it.

With Zachary still in the pack, Bruce went into his bedroom. The air was still, like no one had disturbed it. But he could tell that Mom had been in there because it is was totally dust free, and there was no junk on the floor. His rock posters still decorated his wall, but his desk was cleared, and his shelves were straightened. Weird. Bruce selected a couple novels to read in his spare time—ha, ha, little joke—and returned to the living room. "Are you hungry?" asked Mom. She always asked him that.

He grinned. "Sure. I can always eat."

Mom vanished into the kitchen, and Bruce looked over at his dad, who busied himself with the paper as if his son and grandson weren't even there.

"Do you mind, Dad, if I stay awhile and visit?" asked Bruce.

"No, sit down." Dad's voice was rough, like he wanted to sound casual but couldn't quite manage it. Bruce slipped off the backpack and pulled Zachary out, still sleeping. He laid the baby on the floor, his blanket under him.

Mom reappeared with some heated-up ravioli. "Is the baby okay there?"

Zachary was sprawled on the blanket, one fist in his mouth.

"Yeah," said Bruce. "He sleeps anywhere." Bruce took the plate and began to eat the homemade ravioli. "You ought to open a deli, Mom," he said through a mouthful.

She smiled, running a hand through her hair, pleased.

They talked a little about school, Mom mostly asking questions, Dad listening. Bruce could tell by the long pauses between the pages turning. He didn't tell them about Juliana and Derek. Somehow that wasn't his parents' terrain. At least not now. Maybe when they were more on his side.

"Dessert?" asked Mom.

He didn't want to be a hog. "No thanks. But the ravioli was great." He handed back the plate. "I probably should get going. I've got homework to do."

Besides, Zachary was stirring, and he didn't want the baby screaming. He could tell Mom wanted to hold him. Zachary was pretty cheerful about strangers. But she didn't ask and he didn't offer. Not this time at least.

He put the baby in the pack and shouldered it. "Thanks for the food," he said again and headed for the front door. "It was good to see you both." There. He came close to saying what he wanted.

Mom called good-bye, her voice sorrowful.

Bruce opened the front door. Dad suddenly called to him from the living room. "Wait."

Bruce pulled back his hand.

Dad appeared in the hallway. "I'll drive you back to Justin's," he said.

"You don't have to. I don't mind walking—"

Dad cut him off like he hadn't heard him. "Let me get my wallet and keys."

Bruce grinned to himself as Dad gathered up his stuff. Then he and Dad went out to the car. Even though there was no infant seat, Bruce wasn't going to protest. He strapped himself in, the baby in his lap. Zachary looked around, wide-eyed, and stared at Dad. Bruce tried not to stare too.

Maybe Dad was changing?

Bruce wanted to shout with joy but *quietly* answered Dad's brisk questions about school, caring for Zachary, and Uncle Justin. He knew Dad wouldn't understand about change and hilarity and God being on their side.

Not yet anyway.

CHAPTER 28

Malena

MALENA STOOD STILL. Why was it that the bathroom was always colder than any other part of the church? Nadine didn't look at her but went to the sink and washed her hands. She wore the red sweater that Malena had wanted to keep. She had to admit that Nadine looked much better in it than she did.

Nadine tore a square of paper towel out of the machine and wiped her fingers. Then she met Malena's gaze.

"You look good in that sweater," said Malena. "I'm glad you have it back."

Nadine raised her eyebrows as if to say, Of course I look good in it.

Malena shifted her weight, unsure how to ease into her question. There was no easy way, so she just plunged in. "So what did you tell Angel about us?"

Nadine's lips quirked in a smile. "So this is why all the attention."

Malena shook her head. "I returned your stuff before I knew. But on our way over yesterday we saw Juliana and Derek leaving your place."

Nadine didn't deny it. "How did that Bruce guy get mixed up with her anyhow?" she asked.

Malena shrugged. "How do any two people get together? Lust at first sight, I guess."

"Did she really burn him all over his body?"

"Not exactly. Only on his arm. We got there in time."

Nadine half smiled. "Malena, the rescuer," she said. "Did you know sometimes people don't want to be rescued?"

Malena clenched her teeth. "I'm not trying to rescue you, Nadine." But like a light snapping on, Malena knew that if Nadine would let her, she would still try. Is this what people meant by being a sucker for love?

Malena watched Nadine layer on her lipstick and tried to calm her own trembling.

Nadine pursed her lips and snapped shut the lipstick tube.

"What's coming down, Nadine?" asked Malena. "We were friends once. Would you tell me?"

"Friends, yes," said Nadine. "One of my stupider mistakes."

This was hopeless. She might as well just go back. Mass must be nearly over anyway. She pushed at the door.

Nadine tossed her hair. "Don't have an attack, Malena. I told Angel that he shouldn't get involved."

Malena didn't quite believe her, but she let the door shut and waited.

"Because this isn't Metal Jungle business. Juliana is just looking for an angle, a connection, and that happens to be me. I don't like it. I told her she better find someone else to do her work. You know I hate being used."

Malena knew. She chewed on a strand of her hair.

Nadine stared at her. "You really thought I told Angel to get you, didn't you?" Her voice echoed in the tiny bathroom. "So I had Malena Castillo running scared, huh?"

"Can you blame me?" asked Malena quietly.

Nadine slammed her fist against the metal paper towel holder. Malena jumped.

"I thought you knew me better than that," said Nadine. "I'd never turn the Metal Jungle against you." Nadine stopped abruptly.

"I hoped you wouldn't, but I just didn't know for sure," said Malena. "I had thought I knew you, but—"

Nadine shouldered her purse. "Yeah, well, I guess you really didn't, did you?"

Suddenly Malena felt as if a small heater popped on inside her. "I guess not," she said. "I'm glad I was wrong."

"You always were crazy," said Nadine. She gave her an old, infectious grin. "We've had some good times, no?"

Malena nodded, not daring to talk.

The bathroom door creaked open. A nun stood there, solid, formidable. "Girls, get back to mass. Right now."

Leave it to the nuns. They heard and saw everything.

Malena and Nadine walked back into church, not quite touching.

The final prayers were being said. She and Nadine slipped back to their pews without saying good-bye. Maybe that was good.

Malena sank to her knees between Mama and Lucia. The chant of the prayer closed around her.

Had God changed things?

Maybe, she thought, *he had it all under control the whole time.*